THE
LITERARY DISCIPLINE

THE
LITERARY DISCIPLINE

By

JOHN ERSKINE

Essay Index Reprint Series

BOOKS FOR LIBRARIES PRESS
FREEPORT, NEW YORK

First Published 1923
Reprinted 1969

STANDARD BOOK NUMBER:
8369-1257-8

LIBRARY OF CONGRESS CATALOG CARD NUMBER:
74-90635

PRINTED IN THE UNITED STATES OF AMERICA

TO
GEORGE EDWARD WOODBERRY

CONTENTS

		PAGE
PREFACE		ix
I. DECENCY IN LITERATURE		3
II. ORIGINALITY IN LITERATURE . . .		47
III. THE CULT OF THE NATURAL . . .		91
IV. THE CULT OF THE CONTEMPORARY . .		137
V. THE CHARACTERS PROPER TO LITERA-TURE		187

PREFACE

The following chapters were first published serially in *The North American Review*, from November, 1922, to March, 1923. For their reappearance in this volume I have made slight changes in them all, and have inserted in the fourth chapter a few paragraphs written for *The Bookman* of July, 1922. The editors of both magazines have my thanks for permission to reprint.

The title of the book will disclose at once the critical theory underlying these essays; they are studies in the discipline which literature imposes on those who cultivate it as an art, and their doctrine is that language as a medium of expression has certain limitations which the writer must respect, and that the psychology of his audience limits him also in what he may say, if he would gain a wide hearing and keep it. To know what can be said

PREFACE

in words, and what effect it will have on
your readers, is the inward art of writing,
much more important even than the man-
agement of a sentence or the shaping of
a paragraph.

I write here of literature as an art.
Since I mean to exclude, as not art, many
books of undoubted importance and of
wide appeal, I must attempt at least to
defend a distinction that to certain readers will seem arbitrary. A book may tell
us of a life we already know about, or of
a life we as yet do not know; the pleasure
it gives us will be of recognition or of
curiosity satisfied. Of course no books
fall absolutely into one or the other of
such extremes, but it is fairly accurate to
say that every successful book does give
us information, a new experience, or
brings back an old experience to recognize. Though both kinds of books may be
equally well written, we are inclined to
ask only instruction from the one kind,
but permanent enjoyment from the other.

[x]

PREFACE

One is a document in history or sociology, in ethics or psychology; the other, as I understand it, is a work of art. If our country has not proved a favorable birthplace for literary works of art, the reason probably lies in our history rather than in lack of able writers. Ours has always been, and still is, an unknown land; the reader of American works has primarily been looking for information about America. The early visitors from Europe wrote us up for the enlightenment of their friends at home, and since our world has changed rapidly, we still write up ourselves, for our own enlightenment. The too brief flourishing of literature as an art in New England was possible only because life there for one moment in our history was so stable that a considerable body of readers had much experience in common; having had their curiosity satisfied as to their own life, they could recognize it and reflect upon the literary portrait of it. But the New England moment in our literature proved an exception, and we are so accustomed now to read novels and poems, not as art, but as bulletins of information from the west, the northwest, the middle west or the south, that we are losing the sense of living art in the New England writers themselves, and are considering them more and more as documents in a past civilization. Since we have so great need of documents, I realize that I prejudice myself with many readers when I say that my chief interest is in literature as art—in the books which reflect the unchanging aspects of human experience, rather than in the reports of our temporary condition.

If literature in our country has suffered from our passion for information, I believe it has also been damaged in our day by a bad philosophy of esthetics which has encouraged the writer to think much of himself and little of his audience. Literature is an art of expression, we say in the old phrase, and it expresses life. But whose life? The writer's, of course, replies the philosophy I happen not to like. No; if a book ever becomes famous, it is because it expresses the experience of the reader. The writer's personality will pervade it, but we must be able to recognize ourselves in it before we can admit that it portrays life truly.

The function of criticism, as I understand it, is to discover, in the past experience of the race, what books have won a secure place in men's affections, and to find out if possible why men have been permanently fond of them. A great critic would be a scientist, observing the behavior of the reader in the presence of certain stories or poems, and recording the kind of effect produced by various arrangements of character and plot, or by different employments of language. Such a critic was Aristotle in the *Poetics*. The art of literature has never had an observer more accurate or more penetrating, and those who return constantly to his

wise pages will understand why I have
quoted him so often, and often have drawn
upon him for aid when I have not used
his name.

I must record my gratitude to two living philosophers also, towers of strength
to those of us who love books as works of
art—George Santayana and Frederick J.
E. Woodbridge. The first has taught me
through his books—are any books more
beautiful than his written in English today? The second has enriched me with
his daily companionship and with those
spoken words, grave or gay but always
wise, which his friends and disciples learn
to save up for remembrance.

And I have offered this book in my
dedication to our one poet-critic in
America who has spent his genius in the
service of literature as art, and as art
alone. I do not know whether what I have
written will be altogether acceptable to
him, and if I put his honored name in
the forefront of my pages, it is not to

shield me from deserved criticism. But writing on this theme, I must bear witness to his leadership among all in this country who in my lifetime have known how to prize the immortal things in great books —imagination, ideal humanity, beauty, and the kind of truth that is beauty. In a day when literary criticism has been contentious and personal, more like a political campaign in a tough ward than anything that Spenser or Sidney or Shelley would recognize as a pilgrimage to wisdom, Mr. Woodberry has written nothing ungenerous or harsh of new arrivals less scholarly, less gifted, less accomplished and less chivalrous than himself. He has

Let the younger and unskilled go by
To win his honour and to make his name.

Indeed, more than anyone else among us, he has kept his faith that youth, given time enough, will discover art as it will find out other incarnations of beauty, and will achieve new miracles in its worship. Twenty-five years ago he taught us to

PREFACE

love the masters in poetry—no easier thing
to do for boys then than it is now. We
have still to acquire his hospitality toward
the future, to look on with his good humor
and sympathy while the immature in the
world of art, as elsewhere, try to rearrange the universe, not knowing that it
has been here for some time and is set in
its ways.

J. E.

THE
LITERARY DISCIPLINE

I

DECENCY IN LITERATURE

I

THE quarrel with indecent art is an old one, and the present discussion of improper books, with threats of censorship, begins to rally itself in two familiar camps—on one side the moralists, showing in the heat of debate less understanding of art than they probably have, and on the other side the writers, showing in the same heat somewhat less concern for morals than it is to be hoped they feel. The censorious seem disposed to suppress on the ground of indecency almost any kind of book they happen not to like; the writers seem at times to argue that all books are equally good, or, at least, should be free and equal. These are the old exaggerations of the quarrel. Yet in two important respects the present discussion is quite novel and more than usually interesting; for one thing, the attack now is less on obscenity, about which there are no two opinions, than on indecency, of which we have at the moment no adequate definition; for another thing, the writers themselves, perhaps for the first time in history, have no definition of literary decency to offer, and seem not greatly interested in forming one.

Censorships are usually exercised for the protection of religious or political doctrine, and whatever may be said against the method, at least in the field of religion or politics the censor knows clearly what he wishes to protect. But if we now would protect decency, we must first define the term. It is not enough to have a moral conviction on the subject; we must have also some principle outside of our emotional prejudices, based on something more lasting than fashion. In the present welter of contradictions and opprobrium it is sometimes thought indecent to wear bobbed hair or short skirts; for the morals of the school, teachers have been dismissed who rolled their stockings below the knee. Obviously, these are not great faults in decency, if faults at all; a good deal of camel must have been swallowed before justice could be done to these gnats. Some of our neighbors wish to suppress certain plays; others wish to suppress the theatre. Some wish to suppress Swinburne and Baudelaire, with one hand as it were, while distributing with the other copies of the Bible containing the *Song of Songs*. A minister of this type, earnest in his work for decency and quite muddled as to what it is, told me that he could not give his approval to the *Spoon River Anthology,* brilliant though it was; he could approve of no book that portrayed fornication. Yet he must have read the story of Lot's daughters and their behavior with their father. He approved of the Bible, and he would probably not call it indecent. What is decency, then, or its opposite?

At this point the writers ought to stand up and answer. In other ages they would have done so; they would have thought no one so competent as the artist to define decency in his own field, and they would have stated their definition from the point of view of art. They would have called it "decorum" instead of "decency", but they would have meant the same thing—fitness or propriety in the particular art they practised. When Milton made his famous plea on ethical grounds for freedom of the press, he went on, as an artist, to say that

[6]

of course there are good and bad books, and when a book has had its chance, it must submit to the judgment of the competent. He was writing in an age when the reader might be expected to have some training in artistic definitions of decorum. If books are to enjoy freedom of publication now, it seems incumbent upon the writers to define the decency of their art, and to spread the knowledge of the definition, as widely as possible, that the competent reader of today may have a standard by which to judge.

II

It ought to be possible now, as it once was, to define decency in terms outside our emotions, not variable with our private taste but fixed in the conditions of the artist's work. When man is inspired by the world he sees to make some lasting record of his feeling about it, and selects a medium to express himself in,—wood, stone, metal, color, language,—he immediately encounters certain problems and difficulties in his medium, certain limitations in it which he must submit to, if he would convey his meaning with precision. The limitations of his medium, therefore, dictate to the artist his first lessons in decorum. For if you will not respect those limitations, you will find yourself saying what you did not intend; instead of beauty, you will convey some effect humorous or grotesque or ugly. It is at least bearable to see actual garments on the wax figures in shop-windows; we dress up dolls. But not even the shop window could tolerate a marble statue with clothes on. When the artist learns that some things, though excellent in themselves, do not come out in his medium with the effect he desires, his good sense and the sincerity of his art compel him to leave these subjects for other mediums. The themes he thus abandons are not indecent in the sense of obscenity or filth, not bad in themselves, but they do not fit his art—or, as writers used to say, do not belong to its decorum.

The decorum of art may seem to the moralist far less important than the decency his own strong emotions feel after, but the moralist is wrong. The decorum of art is the deeper kind of decency, for it is based on lasting principles, and it leads to an understanding of the positive good in art, to beauty, as the moralist's concern for decency often does not. You cannot explain on moral grounds why the glorification of the body in Walt Whitman, let us say, is sometimes disconcerting, yet the glorification of it in Greek sculpture seems not only decent but noble. The artist could explain the matter if he understood the decorum of artistic mediums. In so far as he does not understand it, he adds to the confusion of the arts in our time; he fills our magazines, for example, with photographs of Greek dances, and is himself, let us hope, disturbed by the grotesque contortions he has perpetuated. The dance was probably a graceful flow of motion; of all that flow, however, only a few moments would be in the decorum of the camera—moments of poise, in which

motion might be suggested but not represented.   But the photographer was
charmed by the moments of motion, which
are the essence of dance decorum, and he
gives us a picture of grim-faced ladies
suspended in the air, with frantic gestures
of fingers and toes.

In literature, since the medium is language, decorum is a question of the limitations and capacities of words.   The
great limitation of language is that it
must be heard or read one word at a time,
though most of the things we wish to
speak of in this world should be thought
of or seen all at once, and their true out-
line and their total effect may be dislo-
cated by piecemeal expression.   To represent in language a landscape or a person,
a building or any intellectual architecture,
is, strictly speaking, impossible; we can
merely make statements, carefully selected, about the subject, and trust that

no matter how dismembered in the telling, it will somehow come together again in the hearer's mind, thanks largely to the hearer's imagination. Where the suggestion is so slight and the collaboration so great, the writer is under some obligation to be precise and conscientious in what he suggests. His responsibility might perhaps seem less when he is telling a story; if language is inapt for the portrayal of stationary things having mass, structure and extent, we might suppose it better fitted to the representation of action, which like language occurs in sequence of time. But even in the recital of events, language has to name separately in an artificial order events which actually coincide, and the reader's imagination must put the fragments together again. *"Indeed," replied Mr. Jones*, or, *Mr. Jones replied, "Indeed!"* Neither formula quite represents what happened. In life, when

[12]

we heard the "Indeed!" the sound would tell us not only what was said but also who said it. No wonder the poets have so often thought of the drama as the most satisfying literary form, for when a play is acted, words convey in it all that they can convey in life, and they are aided, as in life, by other kinds of language—by gesture, facial expression, scenery, which speak to the eye while the voice is speaking to the ear.

Because words must be spoken one after another, there are not only some things which are hard to say in that medium, but others which in certain circumstances should not be said at all. No matter how much we select the sounds, our utterance will lay a fairly even emphasis on all the things we name; therefore, if we wish to subordinate some part of the picture, to pass over it with no emphasis at all, we cannot throw it into shadow, as a painter can—we must leave it out altogether. A painter may portray a face half in shadow, so that one ear is barely discernible; looking at the picture you do not see the shadowed ear, and do not miss it. But if some one tells you in words that the ear is in shadow, at once the ear enjoys special emphasis, the opposite of the painter's intention. Or suppose the portrait is not shadowed, but all the features are clear; and suppose the artist has focused your attention on the eyes, or has brought out some characteristic expression. You can attend to the picture exactly as you look at the subject in life—noticing what is important in it, but not examining it otherwise in detail. The head has two ears, but you do not count them. If, however, the writer describes the face as it is in life, or as it is in the portrait, he may speak only of the chief focus or expression of it; he must

[14]

not say that the subject has two ears. If he does so, he will be indecent in his art, and may seem to the original of the portrait insulting in his manners.

All literary accounts of the human body raise this problem, not a problem of squeamishness or puritanism, but of decorum. The classical Greeks seem to have mastered the question either by instinctive good taste or by analysis, as they mastered so many other problems in art with which we are only beginning to wrestle. They cannot be accused of prudishness where the body is concerned; they loved its naked beauty, and in their sculpture they portrayed it frankly, with a serious and unflagging delight. Yet in their poetry they did not portray it; they merely noted the total effect of physical beauty, and omitted details, as we should omit the number of ears in the portrait. In the classical Homer, to be sure, there remained even after much expurgating certain stereotyped labels of the body; goddesses are "ox-eyed", beautiful women are "deep-bosomed." But the phrases are so conventional that they probably called up a general sense of approval, rather than a specific detail, as the word "mortals" calls up to us the general idea of men, rather than the fact of death. Aside from such phrases Homer and the other classical poets suggest the body without detail, trying to render the general effect the body makes in life—its femininity, its masculinity—at the same time avoiding any such attention to anatomical detail as in real life would seem, to the Greek and to us, morbid or clinical. The sculptor, working in another medium, can use the details the poet must omit; when we look at his Apollo or his Aphrodite we see not a naked body but a divine presence. The effect of divinity is not furnished by any anatomical member, nor interfered with by any. The body in detail is before us, but the expression, the something divine we feel, is in the attitude or the character. The wise poet, knowing the limitations and dangers of his medium, tries to reproduce only the attitude or the character. Later sculptors, in the decadence that followed the Periclean age, deserted the decorum of their own medium, and called attention to separate parts of the body— to ribs or veins, neck or breasts. In literature a parallel decadence occurred; the poets tried to give the effect of beauty, not in Homer's way, by avoiding physical detail, but by citing it. They managed to suggest not beauty but sex.

The modern lover of beauty who quite properly wishes to restore the body to its rightful honor and reverence, usually appeals to the Greeks for his precedent. But if he wishes to celebrate the body in detail, he should appeal not to the Greeks but to the poets of the Renaissance. The praise of the body in the Renaissance is sometimes explained as springing from a newly recovered delight in material beauty. It should also be explained as a reaction, on the part of earnest, even puritanical moralists, against other moralists who, they thought, viewed life but partially and cramped the human soul. In our own language, Edmund Spenser and John Milton led in this praise of beauty—moralists both; as in modern times Walt Whitman led the praise, a moralist also, whether or not his detractors admit it. But a moral purpose is a dangerous approach to art, whether you are a critic or a poet. Whitman is perhaps the easiest illustration to begin with. He felt that to the pure every part of the body is sacred, and at its best is a thing of beauty. Had he been a sculptor, he would have proceeded to make statues which probably would have shocked nobody. Working in language, however, he mistook the decorum of the art, and wrote as though he were sculptor or painter, and the result is in those anatomical catalogues from which no beauty emerges, whatever else does. He differs as widely as possible from Edmund Spenser in most things, but in this one matter they are alike. Milton was too close to the Greeks to go wrong, even with his moral impulse to assert the honor of the body; his impassioned praise of wedded love, and his remarks on the glory of nakedness when Adam and Eve first appear in his epic, put no strain on literary decorum. But Spenser's moral enthusiasm for beauty leads to such physical inventories as his picture of Belphœbe, in the second book of the *Faerie Queene,* or of his own bride, in the *Amoretti* and the *Epithalamium*—an accounting of eyes,

[19]

teeth, hair, neck, shoulders, breasts, waist, arms and legs. Many a critic has suggested that his poems have the character of painting or of tapestry, and had he actually worked in a pictorial medium, he would have made the effect he desired. In his portrait of Serena naked among the savages, in the sixth book of the *Faerie Queene,* he followed Homer's method with admirable success. No English poet is more spiritual than he—all the more impressive the indecorum to which his moral earnestness occasionally brought him, and all the more helpful his example ought to be to modern beauty-lovers who fancy that the decorum of an art need not be studied and obeyed.

Through ignorance of decorum in language a moralist sometimes comes to grief in the opposite direction; wishing to indicate indecency, he sometimes through reticence stumbles upon the Homeric method and portrays beauty instead. A while ago a minister of some name, an aggressive defender of decency, preached a sermon on the dangers which at the moment he saw threatening us from the arts. According to the newspapers, he said that if certain theatrical managers could get it by the police, we should have ⸱ show in which a naked woman in one scene posed before a black velvet curtain. Wishing to touch the sulphurous subject as gingerly as possible, he merely suggested the lovely contrast of body and background; those of his congregation who had seen it forgot their moral danger and remembered the Venus de Milo in the Louvre. It occurred to some of them that this material might be indecorous in the pulpit; in the theatre, however—well, they were not unwilling to see it, if it was actually put on.

III

The principle of literary decorum
which applies to the representation of the
body applies also to the allied theme of
sex. The body is a fit subject for literature, but not in detail. Sex is a proper
subject for literature, so long as it is represented as a general force in life, and
particular instances of it are decent so
long as they illustrate that general force
and turn our minds to it; but sexual actions are indecent when they cease to illustrate the general fact of sex, and are
studied for their own sake; like the ears
in the portrait, they then assume an emphasis they do not deserve. This seems to
be the decorum of the theme as great writers have treated it, and this is the decorum

[22]

which men instinctively adopt in discussion, if they have not been trained to think
that all discussion of sex is naughty.
People so trained will call any book indecent which in any way touches the theme.
When *Trilby* appeared years ago, many
of us then youngsters were protected (in
vain) from the lovely story because Trilby
had been somebody's mistress before the
romance began. So to an earlier generation *The Scarlet Letter* had seemed dangerous because Hester Prynne's child was
illegitimate. But neither book had physical passion for its theme, though the force
of sex in life, for good or evil, gave each
story most of its interest and its pathos.
How indecent in the artistic sense, how
indecorous, either book might have been,
we realize by supposing that Du Maurier
had centred attention on Trilby's early
and sordid affairs, before she met her true
love, or that Hawthorne had given us in

detail the experiences of Hester in Arthur Dimmesdale's arms. One has an uneasy feeling that so the books might have been written today; the general fact of sex and its influence would not operate as a colossal force in the story, but would be deduced in an argument or assumed as an hypothesis—modern specialists in sex are so uncertain of its existence—and the focus would have been on the animal behavior of human beings, which the hypothesis of sex would explain. This kind of book is indecent, though it is usually too psychological in manner to disturb the censorious, and entirely too frequent in recent literature to suppress.

We turn for relief to the decorum of great literature. "From the roof David saw a woman washing herself, and the woman was very beautiful to look upon." The painter might give the details of that beauty; the writer could not. But he could continue: "And David sent and in-quired after the woman. And one said, Is not this Bathsheba, the daughter of Eliam, the wife of Uriah the Hittite? And David sent messengers and took her, and she came in unto him, and he lay with her; and she returned unto her house. And the woman conceived, and sent and told David, and said, I am with child. And David sent to Joab, saying, Send me Uriah the Hittite." So begins one of the greatest of stories from both points of view, artistic and moral. Is it too frank for our taste? Would the minister who described so well the naked woman and the black velvet, set this story also before his congregation? He ought to, for it is a masterpiece of decency. David's pas-sion, Bathsheba's acceptance of it and her consequent terror, were important only as beginning the spiritual tragedy; the old writer names the facts and passes on to his great subject. To have begun less frankly would have been to misrepresent life and spoil the moral; to have elaborated the scene of David's love-making would have been indecent. In the same decorum the classical Greeks told their stories; Helen eloped with Paris; Œdipus had children by his own mother; Clytemnestra killed her husband and made her lover king—so much of the fact is necessary in each case to understand the magnificent and tragic consequences; but the Greek poets did not pry further into the details of passion.

There are, of course, unhealthy minds which have developed a mania for obscenity, and at the other extreme of exaggeration there are the unbalanced minds which do not care to admit the existence of sex. But sex, in one form or another, is in the thoughts of most people most of the time, and common folk—and

the great poets—speak of it constantly,
and in the same way. In unsophisticated
society, among sincere and simple men,
the references to sex are at once reticent
and frank; it is recognized and respected
as gravitation might be or as the sea is by
sailors—as a power always immanent, in
contact with which men may be lost or
saved. Gossip in that kind of society may
whisper that such a girl had a child by
such a boy only a month after their wed-
ding, or that so and so is not really the son
of his supposed father. Exactly this kind
of scandal furnishes material to Homer
and to the old prophets in the Bible, to
Dante and to Shakespeare, for sex is one
of the permanent sides of our moral
world. If this treatment of it is essential
to a complete picture of life, the thinness
of American literature may well come
from lack of frankness; but current attempts to correct the thinness by dwelling

[27]

on physical details are seeking frankness in the wrong direction and are but so many offenses against literary decorum. One reason why we cling with such pride to *The Scarlet Letter* is that with all its shortcomings as a novel it bases its great moral vision on just such a complete and decent observation of life as our books do not usually give us.

IV

In this discussion of sex our attention has shifted from the problem of language to the question of the general and the particular in art—that is, from the principle of decorum involving the medium of literature to the principle of decorum involving its subject-matter. This second principle, rightly understood, marks the chief difference between contemporary art and what some of us still believe was the great art of the world hitherto—the best of the Greek, the best of the medieval. When you look at life naturally, in the directions dictated by your spontaneous impulses, it is your own life that seems important, your private fortunes, your personal ambitions. Everything that belongs to you seems peculiar, because it is not natural at first to compare the lives of others with our own. A poet who presents experience from this angle of individuality will always make a strong initial appeal and perhaps a lasting one, since he falls in with our instincts, and this accord will seem to us evidence of something profound. Such a poet, to some extent, was Euripides, who imagined his characters sympathetically from their private points of view, and portrayed for us the egotism of human nature in its most tragic form. It is not fair to say that in his world men and women need only to explain themselves in order to be right; but, at least, after they have explained themselves it is hard to tell who are right and who are wrong. Such another poet is Browning, who represents human nature one individual at a time, always from the individual's point of view. By such a simple and primitive method he obtains effects of obvious richness—he shows how varied life is, since there are so many individuals in it, and how novel it perpetually must be, since each of us is discovering the world for the first time, and how much right there is in every man's cause, once he has the chance to speak for himself. If we had all the works of Euripides, we should probably find in them as rich and varied a world as Browning's, expressed with clearer and more direct poetic genius. Our contemporary taste is rather solidly for this kind of literature—Browning flourishes more and more, and Euripides has been revived; and if you really approve of the individualistic approach to art, it is hard to see how you can call anything indecent. Anything that is natural to any kind of character must get a hearing.

But men can also be imaginative enough to look at life as a whole—first, perhaps, to look out at all other men, and then to stand off and look at all men, oneself included. When you begin to take an interest in other men, you notice of course that their lives are not like yours, not so important nor interesting nor promising, but in their drabness they are all curiously alike; they all, with slight variation, are born, are brought up, fall in love according to their lights, marry, earn their living, have children, grow old, and die. When this uniformity begins to interest you, you are making your first intelligent acquaintance with life; and when you have looked at mankind and included yourself in the picture, when you have admitted however reluctantly that the single addition does not change the total effect, that life is still simple and uniform and that you are less peculiar than you thought—then you have seen yourself at last as one of the human race.

DECENCY IN LITERATURE

To see this calls for imagination and for the Greek virtue which we translate as magnanimity—great-mindedness. The virtue is not to be acquired all at once. We have made a great advance when we can think of life in terms not of ourselves but of moral and material aspects and powers—in terms of youth and age, for example, of strength or beauty or pride. This is the allegorical stage of our pilgrimage in wisdom, no mean stage to reach, though it happens to be out of fashion just now. We are acquainted with it in the old morality plays, especially in the almost popular *Everyman,* and perhaps in Æschylus, especially in *Prometheus Bound.*

But our advance is greatest when we can recognize these aspects and powers in the individuals around us—when our observation includes at one and the same time the general truths of life and the

[33]

particular instances. The poet preëminently master of this sane wisdom was Sophocles, who, in Arnold's familiar phrase, saw life steadily and saw it whole. The point of view which he represented is the most magnanimous, the least egotistical, that art has yet taken, and one would have to think meanly of the race to believe that we shall not return to it, as to the noblest part of the Greek legacy. But Sophocles was only the illustration of a decorum generally practised. In the brief and magnificent period which left us our greatest perfection in the arts, the Athenians thought of the individual as important if he illustrated for the moment the general truths or fortunes of life, but his strictly private fate was insignificant.

This attitude has been explained by saying that the Greeks, having no gift for introspection, took always an objective view of life, but such a formula hardly accounts for all the illustrations of magnanimity. When Athens was in her glory, for example, it was only the public buildings that were glorious; no individual, not even Pericles himself, thought of putting Phidias to decorate his private home. Again, in the *Antigone* Sophocles is introspective enough—as introspective as Euripides or Ibsen himself—but the introspection is concerned with the general theme of piety, of one's duty to blood relations, not at all with the love story of Antigone. She was betrothed to the son of the king who condemned her to death, and the fact proves tragic for the son and for the king, but the love of the two young people is their private business, and the poet therefore does not let his heroine discuss the problem of piety from that point of view.

It was the genius of Shakespeare and of Molière, even in comedy, to preserve

[35]

the same decorum. They show us those aspects of man's fortune which are of interest to all men; of course we are free to fill in the gaps according to our taste in gossip, but the dramatist awakens our feelings and calls our attention only to general experiences and common wisdom. In Shakespeare, *Measure for Measure* is a good example, a noble tragedy and a decent play. It is less glorious than the *Antigone,* obviously, since it shows human nature resisting temptation rather than establishing an ideal, but the grimness of its subject and the fact that it portrays an indecent character do not make it indecent, as some critics think. Its power is its probing into general truths of life, chiefly into the capriciousness of temptation where sex is concerned, and into the various forms of the fear of death.

Claudio, condemned to die and convinced that there is no hope, persuades himself that he does not care to live; but immediately he has a chance to live at the cost of his sister's honor, and he finds himself slipping into casuistry to make his escape possible even on such terms. Here is introspection of the Sophoclean sort, touching the psychology not of a particular man but of all of us. Walter Pater remarked the paradox that Angelo is tempted to his fall by sight of the pure-minded Isabella, the incarnation of virtue. He might have named other paradoxes of Isabella's influence. She fascinates all the men she meets, good or bad. At the end of the play the Duke announces that he intends to marry her himself, and since he gives her little opportunity to dispute this plan, we may speculate how far his motives differ essentially from Angelo's. But Lucio, the wretch so steeped by habit in indecency that he can hardly frame a clean sentence, is immediately and permanently sensitive to Isabella's beauty of soul as well as of body. Why? Shakespeare merely exhibits the paradox, in his characteristic way, without hint of explanation. But we may read a lesson in decorum, if we wish, in the decency of art, from the first speech of Lucio to Isabella in the nunnery, when the dirty-minded wretch, having none but coarse formulas in his vocabulary, tries to address her with the reverence he feels.

V

On all this the moralist may comment that decency as a matter of art is one thing, and the protection of public morals is another; that however artists may be interested in the decorum of their medium, or in the general truth of their subject-matter, the public is also interested in the motives and the possible effects of their writing. Granted; but if the moral point is to be made, as against the artistic, the artist has his own conclusions to draw. The first is that one may as reasonably question the motives of the vice-suppressors as the motives of the artists. Better not to question the motives of either, but if the mean insinuation begins, it must in justice spread in both direc-

[39]

tions. The woman before the velvet curtain, described by the preacher, seemed a vision of loveliness; yes, you may say, but what would be the motives of those who produce such an exhibition—worship of beauty, or wish to capitalize our baser impulses? The question is unanswerable unless you can see into men's hearts, but it applies also to the minister who preached the sermon; was he interested only in morals, or was he capitalizing to some extent our craving for the sensational? An artist would be content to answer that where the result is beautiful, in the decorum of the art, it is sensible as well as kind to suppose men's motives of the best; and when the result is not beautiful, it is sufficient to condemn the result, without reference to the motives.

But the more actively censorious hold that the weak need to be saved from themselves; that a constant brooding upon indecencies is the death of the soul. Well, if it is obscenity that we war against, by all means root it out, for it can be recognized at a glance, and the reformer need not brood long upon it. But in the realm of art in which decency rises, the suppression of indecency involves as much brooding on it by the reformer as by the endangered public—in fact, the reformer must specialize in such brooding. Whether or not it is to the death of his soul, it seems to be to the impairment of his taste. You cannot give all your time to bad art and know much about good. The rôle of the censor would take on some dignity if there ever were a censor who was a connoisseur, who was the patron of good poets and painters, who actively supported a clean stage. But then, if you had the taste for the best, no inducement whatever would make you give your life to the detection of indecency.

Human nature is wiser in the long run than any censor; in the long run the books of the highest decency hold their place in fame by crowding out the others. The public suppresses indecent books by reading decent ones. Every artist would respectfully suggest this method to all censors. Perhaps the censors will say that the method is too slow—that it takes too long for the good books to crowd out the others. It does take too long now, but why not hasten the process by calling attention to the good books, instead of delaying it by advertising the bad? If the energy which now tries to suppress books sure to be forgotten in fifty years, were directed to the encouragement of the few books which after fifty years might still be worth reading, the final verdict of fame might be hastened. But there seems to be a decorum in morals too, or perhaps

DECENCY IN LITERATURE

two decorums, a creative and a negative—
one seeking to displace evil by a positive
good, the other too much preoccupied with
the evil to notice the good at all.

.

ORIGINALITY
IN LITERATURE

II

ORIGINALITY IN LITERATURE

I

IF we accept the doctrine of criticism today, originality is a great virtue in a writer, and if we believe the book advertisements, all the new writers as they appear, and as they reappear, have this virtue to a striking, even to an explosive extent. But with all their originality, some of the new books turn out to be dull, and if we reconsider for a moment the books men have finally judged great, we observe that they were rather destitute of the kind of originality we talk of nowadays.

"In poetry, a new cadence means a new idea", wrote the imagist some time ago, defending the use of free verse. The doctrine was in the interest of the cadence, but it implied something larger and more significant, that in poetry newness of ideas is desirable. More recently, an American critic remarked, in effect, that what Lytton Strachey has accomplished in his literary portraits is nothing but what Gamaliel Bradford accomplished in his, and since Mr. Bradford's portraits came first, they should have the credit and the praise which an undiscriminating world bestows on Mr. Strachey's. If the question of priority is raised in this kind of writing, perhaps something should be said for Plutarch; but are we sure we should raise the question of priority? What arrests us in the remark of the American critic is the undebated assumption that literary excellence derives from doing something before somebody else does it. Is it the business of art to discover new ideas, or indeed to busy itself much with any ideas, as separated from emotion and the other elements of complete experience? Is it the originality of genius in art to say something no one has ever thought of before, or to say something we all recognize as important and true? As for the mere question of priority, even stupid things have been said for a first time; do we wear the laurel for being the first to say them?

One suspects that the new cadence will persist in poetry only if we like it, and that Mr. Bradford's reputation will outstrip Mr. Strachey's only if we prefer what he wrote, and if by chance we care for neither, then both will be neglected, though one preceded the other by a hundred years. Excellence is the only originality that art considers. They understand these things better in France. There the young poet even of the most radical school will respect the bias of art towards continuity rather than toward novelty, toward the climax of a tradition rather than its beginning; his formula of self-confidence will be, "Victor Hugo was a great poet, Alfred de Musset was a great poet, and now at last I'm here." But in America the parallel gospel is, "Poor Tennyson couldn't write, nor Longfellow, of course; now for the first time let's have some poetry."

The writers finally judged great, so far from sharing our present concern for originality, would probably not even understand it. What is the object of literature? they would ask. Of course, if it is to portray the individual rather than human nature, or those aspects of life which stand apart from life in general, then each book may have something queer in it, something not in any other book and in that sense original; but then the reader, before long, will be looking for peculiarity in every book he buys—it must be, not better, but "different", to use an American term in esthetics; and the writer then who would meet this demand for the peculiar must make a fresh start with every book. What bad luck, they would say, to be forever a primitive, to be condemned, after every success, to produce something in another vein, the first of its kind. Originality in this sense will be continually undermined by fame, for the more an author is read, and the more people become accustomed to his world, the less he will seem original. On the other hand, if the reader looks for originality, there will be no fame, for no matter how popular an author is, we shall read his book only once, and then be waiting for his next novelty.

But if the object of literature is still, as it was for the great writers, to portray human nature, then the only new thing the artist will look for is a greater success in his art. Human nature is old and

unchangeable; he will hope to make a better portrait than has yet been made—
better, at any rate, for his own people and
his own age, and if possible better absolutely. There is nothing new about religion or love or friendship, war, sunsets,
the sea, danger or death, yet something
remains to be told of each eternal theme,
and when a book comes which tells the
whole, which satisfies some hitherto unex-
pressed yearnings or defines more sharply
something hitherto half-seen, then that
portrait of human nature serves our purposes until we have a still finer, and other
versions meanwhile are neglected and forgotten. We remember how many accounts of Romeo and Juliet there were before Shakespeare told the story to suit us,
and how many records of the journey to
hell before Dante told us the whole truth
of that pilgrimage; perhaps we know the
many desperate attempts, long since mer-

cifully swallowed up in oblivion, to portray the American Indian before Fenimore Cooper made the picture the world wanted. The achievements of literature are all, as in these instances, a gradual reworking of traditional or popular or folk material, and in the process it is precisely because the subject is not original that the audience can decide how well it has been portrayed. A sequence of writers interpreting life are therefore like a succession of virtuosos playing the classics, each trying to give us the true Bach, Beethoven, Chopin, Schumann. Their renderings will be different enough, but the music is the same, and we know it by heart. The player who calls our attention to most beauty in it, will be original or unique in the only way that art permits.

The example of the musician may not seem to all writers a fair parallel; they may protest that the writer creates, as the

composer does, but the player only interprets what is already created. But they
are wrong, and the parallel is correct.
The writer does not create as the composer does. Music is an ultimate pleasure
in itself, like the taste of sugar; so long as
it delights us, we do not ask what it means.
Moreover, since there is no question of its
meaning, we may not need a previous experience to find some enjoyment in it; it
may be satisfactory at first contact. Of
course every art gives a more subtle pleasure as we become practised in appreciat-
ing it, yet the contrast between music and
literature remains a real one, since without any knowledge of life at all men and
even children often penetrate deeply into
the heart of music, but without some
knowledge of life they are stopped at the
very threshold of literature. The key to
that door is some first-hand acquaintance
with life. Music has no other subject-mat-

ter than itself, but literature has life for its content, and to find one's way about in it, we must recognize what it is dealing with. Life is a music already composed. It has been here a long time, and had become already an ancient history when the first poets began to play upon it. They merely said for us the things we had been vainly feeling after, they brought out the colors our eyes had almost missed, they defined sharply the flavors and the half tastes that had haunted us. The amateurs in the audience listen spellbound when the master plays to perfection a piece they have struggled with; this is more to them than the loveliest of new sonatas, for it is their own world in a better light. So mankind will listen to the authentic poet who completes their half-realized selves; and will say of him, somewhat with the woman of Samaria, "He told me all the things that ever I did."

[55]

If the audience enjoy the music best when they have tried to play it themselves, they love it next best when they have heard it often, and they like it least, sometimes not at all, when they hear it for the first time. The reader likes poetry best when he has lived what it interprets; next best when he has heard often of the adventures it renders; least, even to the point of detestation, when he never entered that region of life at all, not even by hearsay. In such a predicament the real ground of his objection to the art is that it is original, at least so far as he is concerned, but the experience of his discomfort will hide the cause of it from him; not himself but the art will seem to him inadequate—is he not as much alive as any one ever was? The book, he will say, portrays a world that is dead. Let us start fresh and be original; let us portray my world.

II

In the slow fermentation of human societies, as fresh elements work their way to the top and for a time give their flavor to history, the new arrival is likely to herald himself in some such terms in a protest against the art which, because he has as yet no share in it, seems to him old and worn out, and in a cry for original expression which to those with a longer memory of the world will be quite familiar. There have been new arrivals before, and their wish to start fresh is the cause rather than the result of decadence. For it is only in a figure of speech that art declines or prospers—it is the artists who are less competent or more so than their predecessors, and the poet who tells us that the

period before him is at an end, is really
proclaiming that he cannot improve upon
it, and if the other poets are like himself,
the preceding period is indeed ended.
There is no other reason why the great
moments of literature were not prolonged.
Shakespeare was better than his predecessors, but he was not perfection; why
did not the drama continue to develop?
Ben Jonson, being himself a new arrival,
and being, for all his book learning, outside the spiritual regions which Elizabethan drama had mainly portrayed,
thought of course that a new kind of art
was needed. He is in danger now of sharing the ignominy of all writers who coming after greater men pay homage through
jealousy. Tennyson was not the greatest
of poets; why did not his successors treat
him as though he were a Greene or a Marlowe, and make Shakespearean improve-
ments in him? To hear the critics of today

rail against his art, one might suppose he had hopelessly damaged the language by using it, or that rhyme and meter had come to a bad end at his hands. The poet who talks this way about his predecessors is never the one who is conscious of the power to swallow them up. If Shakespeare had been a little man, he would have taken one look at Marlowe's *Faustus,* and given up the Elizabethan drama as a creaking and antiquated machine for moral doctrine. Had he been really ignorant of the long-stored-up energies and impulses which were coming to action in his marvellous hour, had he lacked the instinct to recognize them even when badly expressed, and to express them better, he might have walked the streets of London as the oriental arrival walked in Athens, or as the invader from the north walked in Rome—with a conviction that the day of this sort of thing was over. Nothing would remain but to be original.

If the clamor for originality is strong in the United States, it is, perhaps, because here are many arrivals, and the newcomer not infrequently desires us to change our ways in the interest of his comfort. We have so much good will toward him, and we are so conscious of the fine things the various races may bring to our commonwealth, that we usually hesitate to speak frankly of his qualifications as writer or critic. He often brings a rare aptitude for art, and frequently he desires to write, but writing is the one art where his ignorance of life will handicap him. In painting an eye for color, in music an ear for tone and harmony, may carry him through, but in literature he will write in an acquired language, and even if it were his native tongue, in literature his attitude toward the art will be conditioned

[60]

by his knowledge of life. He will perhaps assert rather vigorously that his
knowledge is superior; has he not borne
hardships and risen above them? Those
who have not suffered, he will say, know
nothing of life. He will think you cold-
blooded if you tell him the better way to
say it—that those who have not suffered,
know nothing of suffering. If he desires
to write the literature of suffering, he is
probably competent, but since he is usually a person of strong energy, with a con-
structive temperament, he does not wish to
write merely the literature of suffering,
nor does he usually wish his children to
repeat his hardship, though he may have
said that only by such discipline comes
knowledge. He usually desires to write
about the world in general, as every one
would write, and for this task he usually
has had experience too meagre or too special. It is only in the United States, after

his arrival, that he most often makes his first contact with the older literature—not of America but of his own land; if he has had the experience necessary for understanding it, he absorbs it eagerly, but if his hardships in his fatherland deprived him of the necessary equipment, he will announce that the old literature is played out and meaningless. He is like the native students in South African schools, who may read the skating episode in Wordsworth's *Prelude,* but cannot get the shiver of the ice or the scratch of the steel runners. Those who have been with us for several generations and who through economic or other causes have missed that rich acquaintance with life which would explain what the great writers talk about, are likely to join the most recent comer in a plea for originality. Their fortunes are to be pitied, but their advice in art is hardly to be followed. No amount of sympathy or admiration for them as human beings will accredit them as critics, for art is long, as we have heard, and the approaches to it are long also; though we may teach democracy fast enough to win our vote after five years, we must know at first-hand youth and maturity, and have a suspicion of what old age is like, in the world the poet writes of, before we can give a fair opinion whether he has written well. But if the newcomer recovers here the adventure of life which his hardships cheated him of in the old country, he will find that the great literature of the world represents that adventure faithfully and vitally; it is merely a question of patience with him, since he is energetic and the upturn of the new world is exciting, and it is hard for him to believe that the old shadows in art of a life he has not yet lived will ever again take living form or pulse again in his imagination.

THE LITERARY DISCIPLINE

A new world, a new life, a new art.
This is the sequence his hopes dwell on,
though every term in it is debatable. Is
there a new world, or a new life, or a new
art? Sometimes we are told that in a new
world life must automatically be new, but
the doctrine is not convincing, for at other
times we are summoned to originality, as
to another duty, by the argument that in
a new world we ought to be ashamed to
lead still an old life. Sometimes we hear
that a new life inevitably means a new art,
and we reflect that if life now differs from
what it once was, we need take no thought
for our originality, for we shall be different in spite of ourselves; even by the old
methods art will achieve something new;
if we would write of love, for example,
we need only tell the truth about the passion as we know it, and since the love we
know is like nothing that ever was on sea
or land, our romance will be like nothing

that ever was in song or story. Why all
this fret about it? And if religion and war
and sorrow and death are all by hypothesis
quite other than they once were, how can
we escape originality when we report them
in the setting of the new world and the new
life? But the fact is that those who call
for originality in art are not quite sure,
after all, that the age is a new one—they
would feel safer if some further vestiges of
the past could be obliterated; and though
they justify a new art by speaking much of
their new life, it is far from clear that they
really think life is new, or at heart desire
it to be so. Social and political systems,
yes—but life? Horrible indeed is the vision of an absolutely original career for
one who loves his fellows and prefers to
take his experience outside a madhouse.
"Your prayer is answered," says the original Apollo, touching the original poet's
ears, trembling with originality: "you will

have always a new cadence and a new idea; neither the language nor the substance of your communications will ever have occurred before in human experience. Your art will be unique and solitary. Nothing that men have done before will you condescend to repeat—neither to sleep, nor to eat, nor to travel, nor to know passion, pain, suffering or peace." The poet, lured by the prophecy, might think at last that he had achieved fame, but Apollo would be there to remind him that his was like no fame achieved before —not like Shelley's or Shakespeare's. He might lose his heart, and in the throes of love might fancy he knew at last the meaning of Romeo's story or Tristram's, but the god would remind him that his was a special kind of love, not like the very ancient impulse that moved the sun and the other stars.

We need some divine reminder that our

true desire is to realize in ourselves the best of old experience—not to find an original life, but to bring on the stage once more as far as possible the old procession of passions, sorrows and delights. The latest of us hopes he is not too late to taste for himself the high flavor of life which those before him talked so much about. If falling in love is a business incidental to adolescence, yet it is immensely hastened by our reading and by what we have heard; those whom the passion does not touch usually worry about their immunity instead of being thankful for it, and anything is better than never to have loved at all. It is not passion entirely that fills the hearts of the lovers brought at last to each other's arms; at least, the single thought with which the two hearts beat may be a triumphant "Now I know for myself." Similarly, however strange it may seem, we welcome sorrow and suffering, or we feel ourselves cheated rather than blest if none of it comes our way. Death, too, is less unwelcome than it might fairly be. At least those who faced it and have been reprieved, often remember that a satisfaction in knowing the worst took some of the terror away. There it was at last, the old shadow that waylays us all.

Desiring to discover for ourselves the well known and traditional experience, we desire at the same time a more excellent version of it than our predecessors have enjoyed. We would love as Romeo did, but we like to think that Romeo never loved so well, and ours is a more wonderful Juliet. Even our sorrows will be greater, if we have our way, for in the intensity with which we explore the old experiences we feel rightly that we ought to equal or surpass other men. We dread the operation for appendicitis, before we undergo it; then we reach the point of satisfaction in finding out for ourselves what the operation is like; then finally we are persuaded that the operation was unusually severe, the worst of its kind. This is the artist in us, trying for distinction. And if with the old material of life we seek the distinction of excellence of statement, our motive is not simply a desire to surpass others, nor a desire to indicate progress, but often it is the hope to report the experience once for all. Art has always a dying part in it, as artists well know— some part which must constantly be restored by restatement. Try as he may to express only permanent things, the artist will include something that is aside from the main purpose, that goes out of date. Of course if an artist deliberately strives to be contemporary, and succeeds, his work to that extent will shortly become unintelligible; later poets will then try their hand at refurbishing or restoring the essential thing in the picture, and incidentally, without meaning to, they will include some contemporary and insignificant material of their own, which in time may precipitate another revision. What we call classics are the lucky masterpieces in which the permanent elements are so many and the transitory so few, that it seems useless and impertinent to revise them.

III

The desire for originality is not new, and explanations of it are old. Some of them are based on the supposed working of the artistic temperament. The artist, it is said, craves expression at all costs, and if the craving is not satisfied in one direction, it will reach in another. If we cannot pour all of our energy into our painting or our music, we may express the surplus in long hair and flowing cravat. This explanation, even if it were true, would imply that the artist desires notoriety rather than expression, for you cannot express yourself unless you speak a language your audience already knows, but eccentricity, which is the extreme form of originality, will attract attention even if

it is not understood. But artists are not
likely to admit that this theory does justice
to their temperament. They will remark
that few of the greatest masters have
been eccentric in their appearance, none of
them in their subject-matter. Like other
men they fitted the society in which their
lot fell, except that they had a genius for
feeling life more vitally than other men.
So many of them, like Chaucer or Shakespeare or Scott, cultivated the art of living
close to their fellows and sharing an average fate, that we half suspect the less
gifted would do the same if they could;
for the artist who is original in dress or
manners is not likely to meet human nature in its normal state—rather, his neighbors will whisper when he appears, and
nudge each other, and he will never see
what manners they use toward those who
are not queer. Poets with an original or
eccentric subject-matter meet the same

fate. Could Poe or Baudelaire learn anything about us if they came among us with
a reputation for the abnormal? Would we
not unconsciously close to them our usual
impulses, in our curiosity to observe their
strangeness? To the artist who loves life
in the sane way of a Chaucer, a Mon-
taigne, a Molière, such a welcome would
be calamitous; rather hide anything that
distinguishes him from others, even the
fact that he can write, if by this caution
he may draw closer to his sensitive race,
and observe the undisturbed mystery and
beauty of natural life.

Indeed, the whole question of originality, this desire for novelty, is in the end
a question of our love of life. In the moments when we love life passionately we
are not likely to get too much of it, and we
do not ask to exchange it for another kind.
When art and politics were creative, in
the heyday of writers, painters, architects

and statesmen who later seem to us almost
solitary in their excellence, there was still
no taking thought to be original; they fell
in love, rather, with the obvious. Colum-
bus made no voyage in search of originality—simply there had been too many hints
and rumors for him to stay at home any
longer. Some very original spirits, we
may suppose, took no stock in his expedi-
tion. For Shakespeare or Molière play-
writing was an obvious task, and an old
one; they may have expected to do success-
fully what others had only tried, but except for the success they aimed at nothing
new. Where great poets have spoken on
the matter themselves, their point of view
is quite clear. At the end of the *Vita
Nuova* Dante announced his hope to write
of Beatrice such things as had never been
written of any woman. Not to write a
new kind of book, for women had been
praised before, as he implied, and there

had been poems of vision and pilgrimages through hell; but his hope was to excel. He determined to speak no more of his blessed lady until he could praise her worthily, and to praise such a woman worthily would be to write such things as had been written of no other. In the same mood Milton promised his great epic—in passionate love of the best before him, and in the assurance of doing as well or better—"I began thus to assent both to them and divers of my friends here at home, and not less to an inward prompting, which now grew daily upon me, that by labour and intense study, which I take to be my portion in this life, joined with the strong propensity of nature, I might leave something so written to after-times as they should not willingly let it die." This is the great manner of the poets. But in the opening words of Rousseau's *Confessions,* to take an opposite example, we have the accent of the modern disease; he would undertake, he said, an enterprise of which there had never been a parallel, and of which there would be no imitation—he would tell the truth about one man, about himself. He promised no excellence except the uniqueness of the subject, for truth-telling, though always desirable, can hardly be important unless the subject is worth while.

Rousseau's book is great in spite of its introductory sentence; his subject after all was not unique, for each of us can follow his example and write at least one book about ourselves; and perhaps he told less of the unvarnished truth than he intended, for being an artist in every fiber of his body, he selected from his experience not his most singular adventures, but his adventures in those realms of experience—in sex, for example—which his readers were surest to understand and find interesting. But with his famous announcement, whether or not he followed it, our malady began. Hence all the poems and novels of autobiography, all the diaries of young men and maidens, old men and children, all the bouquets of verse still showered upon us in which the poet confides his intimate symptoms. In all this there is little to remind us of great art, or of the times in which great art has been made; the resemblance is rather to a hospital or an old folks' home, where the inmates find importance in the fact that they have been there longer than their fellows, or are younger, or a little less blind and deaf. Hence also our difficulty in understanding earlier literature, of a date when not originality but excellence was the aim. When we first read Shakespeare's sonnets or Sidney's, we conclude with satisfaction that the poet was writing out of his heart, in the Rousseau fashion. But when we learn that these stories are works of art, dramatic renderings of life, and that the "I" who speaks in the lines is first of all the hero of the story, whether or not he is the poet too; and when we learn further that much of the material is adapted from earlier poets, used over again as we use old words to make up new sentences—then perhaps our respect for the master vanishes, our ideal is cracked; they were not such original poets after all. It is the defect of our taste. We forget that the oldest phrases, if they have the poetic excellence of being true to all of us, are renewed and become personal in the adventure of each individual. Though Job ought to get the credit, by all modern standards, of uttering that very original profession of faith, "I know that my redeemer liveth", yet the words were too full of possible meanings to remain linked with Job's private misfortunes; being already immortal, they seem never to have been said for a first time. Lover after lover has found in his own passion the meaning of some old song, perhaps "My love is like the red, red rose", which until the passion fell on him seemed sentimental and silly. And Rousseau himself in the *Confessions,* at the very outset of his egotism, of his originality, of his indecorous opposing of the individual to the race, records his boyhood love of an old folk-song— precisely the kind of art from which his doctrine led us away.

But nowadays the desire for originality comes not only from the writer; a certain class of readers also demand it, the kind of person who reads with an eye out for imitations and plagiarisms. That plot has been used before, he says, when two men are in love with the same woman—or, that character is copied from so-and-so, when Pierrot's father forgives the returning prodigal. There are reviewers of this type also, who read their victims into categories, calling this poet Tennysonian, that novelist Meredithian, that essayist Emersonian. Such categories become less definite as we read back into the past, for over the range of a few centuries no plot is new, nor does any writer seem altogether unlike the others. There is such a thing as plagiarism, yet unless one is a fanatic for originality, the question of plagiarism is of no great importance; the world is not interested, and if the author is concerned from whom the play or the plot is stolen, his concern is more for his property than for his art. If his work is stolen unchanged, it is still as good art as it was before; if the thief has mangled it, his plagiarized version will not be so good as the authentic text; but if by luck he has improved on what he took, it becomes his, bag and baggage, so far as fame is concerned. Who were the authors of those songs Burns made over into his masterpieces? Who were those dramatists and chroniclers whom Shakespeare rewrote? The names in many cases can be looked up, but they are of no account. The world feels that the great writer conferred a benefit by improving on the earlier work. What is far more important, the world also feels that the great writer, in improving on another man's work, actually invaded no private rights, for the material of literature is life, and life is no one's private property. After the invention of printing, writers saw the possibility of financial dividends from their works, and plagiarism is an aspect of this financial question, but it has otherwise nothing to do with art. The world in general continues to think of art in the old way, as creation rather than as business, and it quite properly cares little who does the creating, or who afterward receives a money reward. What were Homer's annual earnings? Or was it really Homer? Or who besides David wrote his psalms? We know instinctively that these questions are trivial.

But imitation in art is often more apparent than real. If a poet is in touch with his age, he will write of the subjects that interest him, and other poets in touch with the age will also write about what interests them, and consequently they may all write of much the same thing; they are not imitating each other, but they are enjoying a common pleasure, to which one of them may have shown the way. We often say that the popular writer is trying to catch the favor of the public by giving it what it likes, and in some instances he may be calculating and his motives unworthy. But it is more probable that being typical of his age, he simply likes the same things as his fellows. The Elizabethan Londoner liked historical plays; did Shakespeare write them only to please his audience, or rather did he not share the general taste? The principle here implied will explain why any poets who have an enormous popularity will have also an enormous so-called influence. They are popular because they share the people's taste, and the people therefore find in their work what they like; but if their subject-matter is so popular, many others will be writing of it too. The resulting resemblance is not really an influence, or rarely is; it is a contemporary tendency. The poet who is best in the lot will be remembered. All ran, but one receives the prize. However, those who came in second and third are neither imitators nor plagiarists.

IV

To submit oneself to the impersonal discipline of art is hard for the young. Few young writers are lured into the profession by the impossibility of being original in their craft, or by the excellent chance their best works have of becoming anonymous with time. We can imagine them pleading for the rights of their personalities; what on earth did the old pagan mean by his proud *non omnis moriar*, if his personality was not to survive in his work? For their comfort let us add that personality in art is indestructible. If we have any of it, it will live. And if we mean personality when we say originality, thinking of the author rather than of his subject, then we may add also that genuine personality is original in spite of itself. How hard it is to tell a story twice the same way; how difficult to form anything permanent, even habits; how impossible to get once for all into a rut. A dull lecture, though we hear it a second time word for word, is subtly changed, for we no longer hear it the first time, and "afflictions induce callosities", as Sir Thomas Browne said, and "sorrows destroy us or themselves." The record we buy for our phonograph, though we liked it at first, may empty itself with each repetition, till the charm is gone; even the photograph of our dear ones, framed on the wall, has a tendency at last to merge itself in the wall paper. Whatever is repeated in our consciousness becomes mechanical and unnoticed, or the edge of it is blunted. To restore the sharp edges of impression, to bring back the first flavor of things, is the ideal of life and of art; only strong personality can do it, but where such a personality comes, it is irresistible and undisguisable. It shows up best in those attitudes of life which in other hands have grown drab and sordid; the contrast brings out the genius. This kind of success in life is the art of the actor who plays a long run, and who gives even in the one hundredth performance the impression of a fresh experience. A poorer actor would have needed a new play long before. Or we might say that art is a summary of life—and where will personality show itself sooner than in summarizing? When Lafcadio Hearn lectured to his Japanese students, he followed the reading of each English poem by a brief paraphrase in prose, which usually is the most precious part of his criticism; for in the retelling, his personality emphasized what he liked in the verses. If we could ask Tennyson, Morris, Browning.

ORIGINALITY IN LITERATURE

Arnold and Meredith each to write out a summary of something we all know, we should have five criticisms, and five revelations of personality. And there are more personalities in the world than we may realize; only they waste themselves in the search for the original, when all that is needed is to be sincere.

THE
CULT OF THE NATURAL

III

THE CULT OF THE NATURAL

I

IT belongs with the confusion of esthetics in our time that the same people
who ask art to be original often ask it to
be natural. Being natural would appear
at first sight the least original of pro-
grammes. Even if by originality we mean
personality, yet there still seems some
contradiction in the wish at one and the
same time to develop a strong personality
and to remain in a state of nature. Since
it is the thoroughbred, not the wild animal, that is distinguished from his fellows,
and the cultivated bloom, not the field
flower, that charms by its single self rather

than in quantity, a condition of impulse close to the unsifted accidents of life would seem to promise an art notable chiefly for its volume, its indistinction and its insignificance. But those who ask art to be natural never mean completely natural. In their wiser moments they are only asking art not to be artificial, or at least to help them forget it is artificial. They demand a "realistic and romantic naturalism", or "a world of honest, and often harsh reality", and what they are looking for is indicated by the fact that they find something convincingly lifelike in a drama of low life or an American vulgarization of a French farce, but something strained and mechanical in a comedy by Sheridan or Oscar Wilde. Art, no doubt, is still desirable in literature—art shot through with crude material, to reassure us that we are human. Since all plays are highly artificial, naturalness is hardly the word for the virtue of good plays; they are convincing, rather, they take us frankly into another world, and for the moment make us forget it is not our world of everyday. Yet those who ask the stage to be natural are apparently reassured when through the imaginary world of art breaks some accent of ordinary speech, some aspect of our common sordidness. Here, it seems, we touch earth and are strengthened.

The cult of the natural at its best asks of the medium of art also, as well as of the subject, that it wear a common aspect, untouched by artifice. Many of the new poets take as their ideal "the sequence of the spoken phrase", with a special dislike of all "inversions"; the "language of common speech" will serve their purposes. Yet most of them are better poets than their theories would indicate, and their practise, like Wordsworth's in a similar predicament, is perhaps sufficient guide to the kind of naturalness they are after. *An Extempore Effusion upon the Death of James Hogg* is the kind of naturalness Wordsworth fell into when he was off his guard. "Other poets", says a more modern cultivator of naturalism, "will come and perchance perfect where these men have given the tools. Other writers, forgetting the stormy times in which this movement had its birth, will inherit in plenitude and calm that for which they have fought." Most of us who are convinced that all speech is artful in so far as it is intelligible, can occasionally put up with a bit of fine writing like this, but we note in passing that "perchance" and "plenitude" are not the language of common speech today. As for the fear of inversions and the sacredness of the natural word-order, it is enough for the moment to observe that no one order is natural for all peoples, nor for any one speech at all times; different word-orders express different states of emotion, even different ideas, and one is as natural as the other. "Tell me not in mournful numbers" or "Tell not me in mournful numbers"— which is the natural order? From another and contemporary New England poet, who sticks valiantly for the natural sequence of speech, we may examine a characteristic line, which has as high a percentage of nature in it as absence of art can insure—"I must pass that door to go to bed." Would it be less natural to say, "To go to bed, I must pass that door"?

To practise artifice and yet to seem spontaneous, to be natural and yet to achieve art—these ancient paradoxes against which the cultivators of the natural arrive, in both the subject-matter and the medium of literature, need to be examined in greater detail, but it is well to observe them first in a general way, in order to mark how much confusion lies on the very surface of such thinking. It is emotion perhaps rather than thinking; it is a protest in another form against what seems old and inherited; it is an impatience with art itself. Yet art exerts its old charm upon us all, and the worshipper of the natural succumbs unawares to every triumph over nature. In American letters we fix on Abraham Lincoln as our type of natural expression; the legend of his humble beginnings and the plainness of his manner deceive us into a conviction that he was less indebted to art than Thomas Jefferson, and we therefore talk of the rhetorical extravagances of the Declaration and contrast them with the Attic simplicities of the Gettysburg Address. Perhaps we see a final proof of our sound taste in the story that Matthew Arnold

gave up the Address for lost when he got
to the colloquial "proposition"; "dedicated
to the proposition", we say, was more than
his artificial spirit could bear. Whether
Arnold expressed such an opinion, or
whether he would have been right in so
doing, is of less consequence than our
emotional readiness, if we cultivate the
natural, to accept the Lincoln speech as an
illustration of our ideal, and to set it over
against the artifice of Jefferson's great
document—to detect a literary manner in
such a phrase as "When in the course of
human events", and nothing but naturalness in "Fourscore and seven years ago"
—or to find an empty and sounding rhetoric in "life, liberty, and the pursuit of
happiness", but only the democratic syl-
lables of common sense in "government of
the people, by the people, for the people."
Both documents are as rich as they can

[97]

well be in rhetoric, as all great oratory is, and of the two, Lincoln's as a matter of fact is rather more artful in the progress of its ideas.

II

Our confusion in the search for the natural in art springs from the many different
meanings that attach to both words, art
and nature. For most of us, perhaps, art
is a decoration, something supplementary
to life; in the spirit of this definition we
understand what it is to cultivate the arts
—to buy pictures when our means will
permit us that addition to more primary
interests, or to attend the opera after the
preliminary stages of our social pilgrimage. We use the word art so often in this
bad sense, with the implication of insin-
cerity, that there is something bracing in
any invitation to return to nature and to
be once more what we were while we still

were honest with ourselves and had a sense of humor.

This nature that we return to, haunts our thoughts as a fixed state in which the wise soul can find enduring refuge. Just how we get the idea that nature is stable, is not easy to see; the notion often exists in our minds side by side with a deep conviction that life is a flux, and that time and space are but relative terms in the universal stream. But perhaps it is the outer appearance of the world, nature as landscape, that first suggests a refuge even against time, mountains are so immovable in their mysterious silence for us as for Wordsworth, the ocean is so untamable for us, as it was for Byron. Perhaps also the contemplation of the changing universe during the past century of daring and imaginative science has endowed nature with a romantic career of its own, such as the old humanists ascribed only to men;

perhaps the progress of stars, planets and
solar systems, observed or guessed at, suggests in spite of the evolution it illustrates
a deeper kind of rest in the laws by which
that evolution conducts itself; so that the
last result of turning from human art to
watch the behavior of inanimate things is
the conviction that nothing is really inanimate, but that all move in the wisdom of
an art superhuman, in an order peaceful
and eternal as only a divine vitality could
conceive. When we think of nature in
this sense of the word, leaving man out of
the picture, ourselves too as far as possible
who do the thinking, we are ready to say
with Emerson that art is an impertinent
intrusion, nature is all. "Nature in the
common sense refers to essences unchanged by man; space, the air, the river,
the leaf; art is applied to the mixture of
his will with the same things, as in a
house, a canal, a statue, a picture; but his

operations taken together are so insignificant,—a little shaping, baking, patching and washing,—that in an impression so grand as that of the world on the human mind they do not vary the result."

We can speak of nature in this all-embracing way so long as, like Emerson for the moment, we lay aside every thought of man and of the moral world which he creates or brings under his control, and in which his responsibility is fixed. But once we resume that human outlook, we begin to use the word natural in at least two other senses. In the first place we use it to describe the process of life, that constant birth or becoming which seems to have been present to the mind of the Greek also when he used his word for nature— as when Aristotle says, in a famous phrase, that art is an imitation of nature, meaning that the process of art is a copy of the processes of birth and becoming, and creates by the same methods that life does. In this sense of the word nature is like art, not opposed to it, and with this interpretation Polixenes tried to rebuke the cult of the natural in Perdita, who would not have in her garden a flower artificially bred:

Yet nature is made better by no mean,
But nature makes that mean: so, o'er that art
Which you say adds to nature, is an art
That nature makes. You see, sweet maid, we
    marry
A gentler scion to the wildest stock,
And make conceive a bark of baser kind
By bud of nobler race: this is an art
Which does mend nature—change it rather:
    but
The art itself is nature.

We use the word nature also to describe the raw material of life which is the result of a previous birth or becoming. It is what some earlier art, human or divine, has already worked on, and what we must work on now if art is to continue. Nature in this sense is the marble, the color, the language which are to be the mediums of various arts; human passions and instincts also, the social and the material environments which attend our lives, the accidents of fortune which make up their plots; and since all this is what art must work upon, nature so defined is forever somewhat opposed to art, as inanimate materials are opposed to the workman, as the wood and the chisel are opposed to the carpenter. For art is the use of the materials of life for human benefit, a method employed for a premeditated end in a world which except for art might seem given over to chance. Because it is a rearrangement and a control of nature to effect the will of man, life itself, so far as it becomes civilized, becomes an art. But in a world as old as ours the raw material with which art deals is itself the result of art; the wood has been already shaped into boards, the chisel and the hammer have been made into tools before the carpenter touches them, and the environment in which the carpenter is born, the instincts and passions he inherits, the turns and coincidences of his fate, are all probably the result of what others before him made of their materials and opportunities. Thinking of life so, we see it as an alternation of nature and art, or as an alternation in which what first is art becomes afterwards nature, all the achievement of one generation turning into mere starting point and opportunity for the next; and thinking of life so, we understand how nature, to the true artist, is forever set over against art in a contrast that implies affection rather than antagonism, for those who instead of defining art as a decorative supplement to life identify it with civilization itself, are free to love nature without abandoning an ideal, as a sculptor is free to love fine marble, or the painter to love his medium of tint and tone. With time and by such a process of reworking, nature draws nearer and nearer to art; the raw material is made constantly more orderly by rearrangement, as a field is enriched by plowing in the crops. Even in the sphere of human character this is true, in the very seat of the natural, in our instincts and passions; for though we may agree that character should be measured by a moral career rather than by impulses wholly innate, yet it is well to reflect that your impulses and sentiments, if you are born and brought up in Florence or Chartres, Heidelberg or Seville, are likely to be different from the impulses and sentiments natural to a child born or brought up in The Bronx or in Hoboken. In the eyes of the naturalist, nature is all, as

Emerson said, and art only a little shaping, baking, patching and washing, but to the artist who carries in his imagination something of the scope of agelong growth and creation, the truth is what Nature said to the poet in Voltaire's dialogue—"They call me nature, but by this time I am become all art."

III

The possibility, then, of returning to nature disappears when we realize how long a road we have traveled; all that the most primitive minded of us can do is to stick close to the raw material of his own life, to the circumstances with which the art of his predecessors surrounded him. This is the nature which the realists cultivate today. They report those facts of life from which art might take its beginning, but they report them as much as possible in an arrested state, for fear they might pass on into art. Among the poets one, catching the accent of the spoken language, gives us the language of one phase of New England; another, with a like faithfulness to the natural cadence, gives us another kind of New England speech;

a third has the colloquialism of Illinois. They are all artists, or they would not mean much to us, but in so far as they have followed their own ideals of the natural they have laid aside some of the magician's robes to which by inheritance they are entitled, and they leave with us their renderings of our world in a form of utterance less noble than their theme and out of harmony with it. In our prose and verse alike, the studied inadequacy of style to the occasion is a standing reproach to us, all the worse since it is often the pose of an inverted vanity, like the democratic conviction still flourishing in the land that the dinner coat or the evening coat is an artifice of a worn-out society, whereas the senatorial frock coat and wide hat are natural and God-given sheathings of our original nakedness.

To revert to the starting point of our lives is to seek nature in vain, since the alternations of art and nature proceed relentlessly, whether we rest our dead weight on the process or try to help it along. It is a vain flattery of our reluctance to travel, to take our seat always in the last car. But, however futile, the cult of the natural in literature has a reasonable explanation, and it is well to understand with sympathy why it is likely to recur periodically in a civilization that must feel its age more and more. Art criticizes life, as we have often been told, by selecting or sifting it; that is what the word criticism means. The authority that art has over us, its right to make such a sifting, derives not from books but from the human brain itself, from the method of memory; we remember only by forgetting most of the things we have done or have suffered, and rearranging the rest. As we grow older life becomes clearer, we say, thanks to this selection and forgetting.

When art sifts life, then, it is only imitating the process of nature, and when we observe the process we can understand why the Greeks said that memory was the mother of the muses. But this sifting of life on the part of memory and of art is progressive, and in all honesty we may wonder at times whether it has not gone too far. Some of the clarity of vision, the firmness of doctrine, which is the reward of old age, may be not the genuine harvesting of experience which is almost the gift of prophecy; it may be rather a partial memory which seems clear because so much has been left out. If a poet could get a first-hand impression of life, his art would be one sifting of nature; if he reacts not only to nature but to the interpretations of other poets, his art is a second sifting, more highly organized, perhaps, more intelligible, than is normally recorded from immediate contact with life. It makes no difference whether we call these siftings poetry or criticism, since poetry, as Arnold reminded us, is a criticism of life. The poet may submit his sensitiveness to nature as sifted through three or four or any number of interventions of personality, and we may call the result poetry, or criticism, or criticism of criticism; very often we cannot tell, and the poet does not know, whether the life that stimulates him is direct or transmitted. But in each remove from the first contact with nature, in each additional intervention of personality, we get a clearer order and a finer intelligibility—truth instead of facts, formulas instead of experiences, and fewer exceptions. The literature, then, which begins in naturalism will at last emerge in philosophy, if we allow it time enough, and the biography of an individual will be condensed and generalized into a proverb.

THE CULT OF THE NATURAL

There are two good reasons, however, for suspecting this economical result. One is that the proverb is probably not true. To arrive at it, in each successive sifting we have left out something, and the total of all the omissions has become almost as comprehensive as the original experience. We must go back and gather up the discarded fragments of our adventure, in order to qualify properly our too simple and absolute summary of life. The art of the historian, we often fear, progresses by some such over-elimination; archæology sometimes rescues him by restoring large sections of a past, the absence of which he had not noticed, but in periods too recent for archæology to take him by surprise, he constantly rewrites his history, to sift it more to his mind, until we may suspect that his account is nearer to our philosophy than to the original facts. In history this tendency is hardly a matter of concern, for if we have a criticism of the eighteenth century which satisfies us, we are content, and the eighteenth century, being dead and gone, will not mind; the poet, therefore, can look on with equanimity while the historians propose to rewrite our national life in order to bring it more in harmony with our present sentiments toward this or that other country; the poet knows that history is not a science but one of the most fascinating of the arts, closely allied to eloquence in its mission to teach and persuade, and that having to do strictly with the past it enjoys rare freedom in sifting its facts. But the poet himself enjoys no such freedom. Whatever he writes will be checked up by the life we now live; his readers will look into their hearts and criticize. If therefore he has gained his clarity by leaving out things essential in our experience, we reject him as too far from our reality to be of consequence to the race. He may be a philosopher; he is no poet.

His philosophy may even be true, and yet his right to the laurel may be justly denied. For the special service of art is to make us live more intensely in the very life which art sifts and selects—in fact, the sifting has for its conscious purpose a more vivid realization of what we live through, and a novel or a play is successful, from the standpoint of imaginative literature, only in the degree to which we enter the work, become ourselves the hero, fall in love with the heroine, hate the villain. In this sense the dime novel and the melodrama, though carelessly branded by the theorist as bad art, are likely to be very good art indeed, and the over-reasoned story, though adorned with subtle reflection and refinements of diction, is in fact poor art, as the average person in his heart knows, for in such books the reflection upon life is paid for by a failure to represent what the reflection is about. If the author would only share with us the adventures that caused him to reflect, we could do our own reflecting upon them, but if he will not share the secret which inspires him, we do not care much what philosophizing he does. Literature continues to be great so long as the sifting it makes it really a selection only from life, and what remains is for the imagination still a first-hand experience; when the residue grows thin to the imagination and addresses itself rather to logic, we feel justified in making whatever return we can to our starting point in nature, to reassure ourselves there, if we cannot in the book, that this human life we love is still with us.

IV

If such a taking to cover is observed in much writing today, the writers who in one form or another now cultivate nature rather than art may plead with justice that the best literature our country produced before them was perilously deficient in a sense of reality. If they do so plead, however, they ought to be consistent. If they think that so great an artist as Hawthorne was deficient in reality, that transcendental philosophy occupies too much room in his romances and the sense of actual American life too little, then they ought not to tell us at the same time that Poe and Whitman are our great poets, for those two were even further along toward

[117]

the abstract than Hawthorne. And there
will be an increasing obligation on those
who in each generation of the fast-ripen-
ing world make a return to nature, to pro-
vide some demonstration that it is not life
after all they are running away from.
Some men have taken to the hermit's cell
to find God; others to avoid responsibility.
As civilization becomes greater in quantity, with more discoveries of science, with
more apparatus of education, we need
more and more the poetic genius that will
dedicate this material to great ends, and
by articulating for us what we can recognize as our best ideal, teach us to simplify
life by casting off the other less significant
interests. The solution of all this raw
material for art can only be a greater art.
When we turn back from this heroic opportunity to take refuge in what is for us
nature, we must convince ourselves, if we
can that our retreat does not indicate

in us inadequate equipment or weak nerve or small heart.

In our present cult of the natural there is cause to suspect some such lack of skill and courage. The plea that our predecessors were so deficient in reality that we, to save the day, must exhibit less art than theirs, will not go in the long run. Our new poetry is curiously relaxed and enervated in temper, ground-hugging, grey and flat; if we have moods which such writing adequately represents, we have other moments more cheerful and creative, which our architecture and our engineering manage to express, but which cannot be guessed at in our poetry, not as much as the oak can be guessed at in the acorn. Our novels, too, have lost their courage, and though they often represent photographically the machine of civilization which builds up around us, and which now is the raw material on which our art is to operate, they do not even attempt to portray the spirit of the artist which actually pervades the land, the joy in putting the machine to human uses, the almost divine ecstasy in having made so much of nature subject already to the mind. This mood of confidence in art is as much a fact in our national life as the number of gallons that flow over Niagara each hour, but the poets and novelists seem to have taken fright.

In both verse and prose, in style as well as subject, the cult of the natural has limited our writers to a few individualistic attitudes, and has taken from them the power to speak with authority on all subjects for us all. We have no American poet, no American novelist; each is the poet or novelist of Vermont or Boston or Maine or Chicago—whatever scene is to him by birth or habit his natural world. To find a universal utterance of universal experience is the aim and the tendency of art, but the cult of nature compels us to return each in what state he came. The counsel to use the language of ordinary speech limits us to the speech of some locality; and such limitation is a fatal handicap for great poetry. The advice to use only the natural word-order limits us to the word-order which each of us finds natural, whereas it is our duty, on the contrary, if we make any claim to mastery in literature, to enlarge our vocabulary even beyond the words our family and our neighbors made natural to us, and to cultivate all the variety of word-order our speech permits, that we may enrich and refine our style, and render our meaning more precise. The temptation to get along with a small vocabulary and a meagre change of construction is altogether too natural; we did not need this premeditated urging to a still greater poverty. Hith-

erto the best remedy for a narrow equipment in language has been to read constantly in the great writers; it was they
who extended the powers of speech and
laid upon each tongue the shape and cadence which to the ill-informed might seem
the gift of nature. But now that the ideal
of the writer is to shrink to the measure
of the conversation he is used to, how shall
our nobler moments find expression? Not
even in reading old authors, for by the
contemporary doctrine of naturalness the
old masters are artificial. "Whither thou
goest, I will go, and where thou lodgest, I
will lodge; thy people shall be my people,
and thy God my God. Where thou diest,
will I die, and there will I be buried."
. . . "At her feet he bowed, he fell, he lay
down; at her feet he bowed, he fell; where
he bowed there he fell down dead." . . .
"Or ever the silver cord be loosed, or the
golden bowl be broken, or the pitcher be

broken at the fountain, or the wheel broken at the cistern. Then shall the dust return to the earth as it was, and the spirit shall return unto God who gave it."

These cadences are not natural, and they are not modeled on the sounds that habitually fill our ears. Their distinction, or if you like, their condemnation, is that they are works of art. Such language gets away as far as it can from time and place, and by much sifting out from unessentials it tries to preserve a universal appeal. If you can write this way at all, you can write as well in New York as in London, as well now as in 1611.

The purpose of art is to make its subject-matter also universal, to sift and rearrange the raw material of life into a history that will have as much meaning as possible for as many readers as possible, for as long as possible. But the cult of the natural tends to the opposite effect—to make the subject-matter of literature temporary in its interest and limited in its meaning. The Broadway entertainments which please us for the moment, since they conform to our taste in the spontaneous, the impromptu and the natural, are but the raw material of drama; good plays might be made out of them; but in each case the author stops the story before we pass from nature to art. It is natural, in the sense of our definition, that a stoker in modern times should have two ideas— that to the idle and effete he may seem akin to the missing link, and that since he is at the bottom of society, he must be supporting it. Quite a philosophy can be made out of two ideas, and these two, when put together, as in a recent drama, promise an explosion. But after all, nothing explodes. The man simply enunciates his two ideas in different accents of violence, until the author thinks it is time to stop, and gets him strangled in the zoo. An artist would have been interested to see in action a character with such a philosophy. We have recently seen another play with an idea, a very simple one; by any means in her power a girl is going to capture the man she loves. Since the only means in her power are eccentric ones, we watch her eccentricity with astonishment for three acts; her behavior is original, like nothing that ever was or will be, and our interest is held by the growing desperation of her ingenuity. Well, she gets him—for much the same reason that the philosophic stoker was strangled, because it is time for the audience to go home. An artist would have granted her ambition as natural, and her success as natural too; he would have shown us, however, what happened after her success, when her philosophy of opportunism in etiquette would have met its

test. Had *Much Ado About Nothing*
been written by the author of either of the
plays just described, the famous comedy
would never have got further than the raw
material of the story, the legend that
Benedick and Beatrice waged a merry war
between them; we should have had an evening's entertainment of jokes and insults,
made gradually more intensive, more vio-
lent and more surprising in order to hold
us till the last curtain. Shakespeare,
choosing the way of art, begins rather at
the point where the wit of Beatrice and
Benedick is exhausted; they have the
reputation for it, but their public efforts
show signs of strain and flagging. From
this start in nature the play proceeds to
represent what happened to Benedick
and Beatrice, the witty enemies, when
serious accidents brought their fates together.

V

Nowhere in literature, perhaps, is art so obviously essential and naturalism so obviously fatal as in drama, for drama, by exhibiting life to us directly, quickens to its utmost whatever desire we have to see our fellows move on from their natural beginnings to some achievement or significant conclusion. Impulses, ideas, motives, prejudices, passions, and as we now say, complexes, are all natural forms of energy; in real life they weary us if they have only a lyric expression, and we wish they would get started into action. Their attempts toward action may be thwarted, and such a defeat may be tragically significant, but at least they should try, and if instead of trying they waste

themselves in talk, they become not energies but nuisances. It is for this reason,
we suppose, that Aristotle long ago cau-
tioned us that tragedy, or all drama, is an
imitation not of men but of an action, and
that plot is the essential thing. He might
have said that character may exist in a
state of nature, but plot presupposes art
in life, a selection from all other incidents
of one succession of events which so selected have a meaning. What he did say
was that without action there can be no
drama, but there may be without character. Plot is a generalization of life, in
which the actors may or may not be portrayed as individuals. The woman who
lost the piece of silver, the good Samari-
tan, the mother of Œdipus, are clear
enough in their universal relation to the
story in which they appear; their personalities may be restated to suit our taste,
or left undefined. We read in the news-

paper that a man jumps into the river to save a drowning child, and having got to land, discovers that he has rescued his own son. We live in that drama without asking what was the character of the father or what was the psychology of the son.

It is remarkable how Shakespeare illustrates Aristotle's doctrine, by showing his characters in action and by avoiding as far as possible an analysis of their motives, their instincts, their prejudices, their passions. Life with him finds expression in art or not at all. It is a mirror indeed which he applies to nature, not a microscope; in his glass we see the form of virtue and the features of vice, we know who are good and who are bad, at least as accurately as we form such judgments in life, but we do not know the motives of the good or the bad. What were Falstaff's motives? Should he be acted as a comic or a tragic character? Why did Portia like Bassanio? Why did Cordelia take such an absolute stand with her father? What did Hero think of Claudio, or Hermione of Leontes, after the restoration to the jealous husband? Was Hamlet's mother an accessory to the murder of his father, or did her conscience trouble her only because she had made a second marriage and in such haste? The profundity of Shakespeare's art lies in his genius for representing the surface of action; in art as in ethics, life is chiefly conduct, and it is enough that behind conduct lies unprobed the same mystery that lies behind existence itself.

But since naturalism thinks otherwise, Shakespeare is no longer our example. Browning is more in our vein. For him the natural man, the raw material of each one of us, the hidden instincts and impulses, must be the whole subject, and action he finds useful only in the fragmentary incidents that must be premised before you can conclude anything even about instincts. Few verdicts in criticism are wider of the mark than the too familiar saying that Browning's genius is Shakespearean. He is the opposite of Shakespeare. He is absorbed in what we call in a loose way psychology, in the original man apart from his conduct, or as far apart from it as you can separate him. To be so concerned about motives and instincts is to be a kind of inverted dramatist, moving back from action instead of toward it; it is no wonder, therefore, that Browning's so-called dramas fail on the stage, since in that direct relation to the audience their static naturalness, their inability to live out a significance in conduct, is pitilessly revealed. Everybody examines himself and talks about himself, as God made him; nothing gets under way; the audience is finally delivered by the death of the soliloquizer, not in a zoo, but more politely, it may be, in a gondola. "Even if you string together a set of speeches expressive of character," said Aristotle, "though well finished in diction and in thought, yet you will not produce the essential tragic effect nearly so well as with a play which, however deficient in these respects, yet has a plot and artistically constructed incidents." To return to nature absolutely would be to return to silence. Short of silence, to return to nature in literature is to confess your private character in monologue. Browning is master in that kind. It would be untactful to name the writers today who share the mastery with him, and perhaps it is enough merely to suggest the idea. To save time we might prudently meditate rather upon the few poets and novelists remaining whose art gets further than monologue.

Meanwhile the universe marches on its secret errand, not altogether secret since it marches, and its art is slowly dramatized in its vast conduct. Art for art's sake is a formula inspiring if taken in a noble sense, but in any sense it is intelligible as a programme deliberately chosen. To cultivate nature for nature's sake is absurd. For nature is here without our aid, and to preserve it in what we call its pure state, we need cultivate nothing—unless it be a more animal contentedness to profit in indolence by the art of those who came before us.

THE CULT OF THE
CONTEMPORARY

IV

THE CULT OF THE CONTEMPORARY

I

"THE end of playing", said Hamlet, "both at the first and now, was and is, to show the very age and body of the time, his form and presence." It would seem that Hamlet thought the business of art was to portray the age in which the artist lived, not only to address his contemporaries, but to speak to them about themselves. The cult of the contemporary, then, in our own day could ask for no better text than this phrase of the Prince of Denmark; what a pity he uttered it so long ago!

Shakespeare did not agree with Hamlet

—at least, he made some pretence to show his Elizabethan audience the form and presence of remote times and far-away countries, Rome and Athens, Denmark itself, Italy, Scotland, Bohemia, the age of King John and the Richards and the Henrys, the time and place, whatever they were, of *Midsummer Night's Dream,* the *Tempest, Cymbeline,* the *Winter's Tale.* And Hamlet himself, be it noted, is hardly faithful to his theory, for when he asks the players to repeat a favorite speech of his, it turns out to be Æneas's tale to Dido. It was from a piece, he said, that pleased not the million, perhaps never had a second performance, but in the judgment of the competent and in his own opinion it was an excellent play. Perhaps the million were at the moment bred exclusively to appreciate contemporary themes; costume plays were not the fashion. Hamlet's other choice in drama is poor evidence of his esthetic theory; the murder of Gonzaga seems to have been already ancient history, but he chose it to catch the conscience of the king, since the story fitted his own household tragedy. Shall we follow the hint, and suggest that Hamlet, like Shakespeare, really had nothing in common with those who would make contemporary life the proper subject for art? Perhaps he would not have mentioned the age and body of the time, if he had not just said that the end of playing is to show scorn her own image, if indeed the purpose of his meddling with the drama at all, at that moment, had not been to sting the royal murderer into a confession of his guilt.

The cult of the contemporary follows logically from the cult of the natural. If we are to write of a life untouched with art, we can write only of life about us, as our fathers left it to us—our best of na-

ture, the talent buried in a napkin; and
if we are to use the ordinary language of
men, we must use today's language, the
only speech that to us is ordinary. And
if it is possible to understand the search
for the natural as an effort to correct the
generalizing tendency in literature, we
may also find a sympathetic explanation
of the insistence on the contemporary,
when we recall how many writers have
reasoned themselves into a determination
to walk in the ways of their heart and in
the sight of their eyes. Did not Homer
celebrate the glory of Hellenism? Did not
Virgil celebrate the empire of Rome?
Well, then, we ought to celebrate the
United States, our United States, rather
than the country of Washington or Jefferson; we ought to celebrate the hour and
the place we know, for we ought to love
what we know—New York, Boston, Chicago or the Middle West. This con-

clusion seems rational, but the desired enthusiasm does not follow; the celebration
of the contemporary in our literature is as
dreary in its results as the worship of the
natural, inspired merely by the sense of
some duty rather than by delight in what is
portrayed. Homer's zest for Hellenism
is undeniable, and the instinct is right that
we, too, must love life as he loved it before
we can write as he wrote. For the moment
we postpone the question, whether we
must not also live a life as noble in kind as
he portrayed. Virgil, writing in a more
complicated, a sadder age, none the less
loved imperial Rome, and we are right to
think that before we shall be worthy to
sing of our own land, in its own grave and
complex era, we must take it to heart,
problems and all. "The proof of a poet",
said Whitman, "shall be sternly deferred
till his country absorbs him as affection-
ately as he absorbed it." But Whitman's

own practise is a provoking comment on his saying; he succeeded remarkably in loving his land under an eternal form; the form and presence of his day he did not leave us. His poems are no guide-books to Manhattan and Long Island in 1855; even his beloved ferry-boats are dateless.

In what sense, then, would Whitman have us love our country, the home of our own times, and how did Homer and Virgil, as artists, love the Greece or the Rome they knew? To be of one's age, yet to be immortal, is a problem more subtle perhaps than to achieve an art that seems natural, but it can be solved in the same way, by defining the terms of our esthetic, and by referring them, as to a touchstone, to what we know of our common human nature. The question can also be narrowed at the start, and very profitably, by pressing home our reflections on Hamlet's remark to the players. There is one kind of writing which does confine itself to the feature of virtue and the image of scorn, and which does indeed, for that very reason, limit itself always to giving the form and presence of the time—the kind of writing, that is, which indicts human nature instead of portraying it. Our better selves, our ideals, are of no time, but our faults are personal responsibilities and strictly contemporary. Satire, therefore, which holds up to merriment or to scorn what is ridiculous or base, must always take a present subject, and in general any art that leans toward the consideration of our shortcomings will lean also toward the life enacted at the moment. If Hamlet meant to trap the king, of course he would write into the old play the very murder the king had committed only three or four months ago; this would not be satire in the usual sense, but it would serve the same end, to convict the guilty and to reform the world. The cult of the contemporary, then, is proper quite literally for satire; it remains only to ask how far it is proper for art.

But is satire not art? Did not Martial and Juvenal, Dryden and Pope write highly artistic satires? There is an art of satire, we must answer, as there is an art of preaching and an art of prosecuting a criminal case. But if there is a distinction between art and morals, then satire belongs to the world of ethics, and of ethics on the grim side, rather than to the world of beauty and delight. To survey and judge the morals of one's age is a serious office that no thoughtful and sensitive person seems altogether to neglect; if the purpose of art is to make such a survey, as Hamlet seems to say, then *Twelfth Night* is hardly a masterpiece in art, and *Sandford and Merton* is certainly one. If art, on the other hand, has for its purpose to salvage out of our crude days the truth which can be translated into beauty, and which so translated may be a joy for ever, then art will have as little as possible to do with men's faults—what faults are joys for ever?—and the kind of writing which confines itself to our frailties or our sins will be as far removed as possible from art. Moreover, the moralist desires a cure of souls, and when the fault is remedied, who will care for the satire or even understand it? It is easy enough, without taking thought, to perish with our own time, but it is one of the oldest hopes art has held out to natural man, that being purified into art he should not altogether die. But mortality is germane to satire. When we read Dryden's terrible excoriations of Og and Doeg, we can only wonder who were the human beings he hated so, and when we come to know something of their lives and characters, we are more con-

fused to name the moral impulse in him
which made it necessary to fix them in so
warm a hell. In art, loving your own
times does not mean loving to find fault
with them.

II

A genuine love of your own time is the recognition, in what you meet in it, of those best moments which crave to be made accessible even for the remotest of ages following. To immortalize any given moment, however, is to take it out of the temporary and somehow to find a language for it so general in its appeal that hereafter it may preserve in its own significance the trivial circumstances from which it first arose. Whenever a genuine love of life stirs the artist, it will be a passion for what he thinks is the best in his own day; even if he is antiquarian and takes for object of his devotion some medieval phase of life, it is medievalism in his own day that he worships. Such a passion leads the writer toward the future, for since it is an ideal passion, yet to be realized, he instinctively proclaims it to posterity, or tries to; but in his search for the right language in which to utter it, he as instinctively turns to the past. To cultivate the contemporary in art is therefore as absurd as to waste effort cultivating the natural, for the present, like nature, is always with us; but the problem for the artist is to express a vision which necessarily points toward the future in language which necessarily trails from the past. We cannot remind ourselves too often that even the single words of common speech must be used by each one of us perhaps a lifetime before they are charged with emotions or sharpened to precise meanings, and before the writer can use them with full effect they must be so charged and sharpened for all his readers. The language of poetry, moreover,

is far more than single words; it is chiefly
the metaphors and the legends, the characters and the episodes, which the race has
met with so often that at last they suggest
accurately to all men the same feelings
and the same thoughts. Life at each
moment may be on its way to become
something to talk with, but only the rash
would try to express a serious ideal
through a picture of that life which is still
near us, and therefore still imperfectly
seasoned or digested. The patriotism that
Shakespeare dramatized for his audience
was certainly a passion for the England of
Elizabeth; that is why he expressed it
through Faulconbridge, the child of Rich-
ard the Lion-Hearted, or through John
of Gaunt, or through Henry V. Why did
he not put Elizabeth on his stage, with
Raleigh and Spenser and Drake and Sidney? Was he blind to the glory of his own
hour? He seems not to have been so, but

in his own hour neither the Queen nor any
of her great courtiers was as clear a figure
to the emotions as time has since made
them all; the sentiment of the audience
would be divided as to each one of them,
the adherents to Rome still perhaps cursing Henry's daughter in their hearts, the
friends of Ireland perhaps cursing the
poet of the *Faerie Queene*. But the wise
dramatist was on safe ground, he knew,
when the audience heard their common
love of country issue unprejudiced from
the lips of old Gaunt, who died two centuries earlier:

This fortress, built by nature for herself,
Against infection and the hand of war;
This happy breed of men, this little world,
This precious stone set in the silver sea,
Which serves it in the office of a wall,
Or as a moat defensive to a house,
Against the envy of less happier lands;
This blessed spot, this earth, this realm, this
       England.

THE CULT OF THE CONTEMPORARY

When a poet turns to the past for language with which to express his love of the present or his vision of the future, he soon learns that not all epochs lend themselves with equal felicity to his purpose; he must select that aspect of the past which is adequate in nobility and energy to what he has to say, and he must select that aspect of the past which will be understood emotionally by his readers. We are prepared, every one of us perhaps, to admit the necessity of this twofold selection, but to admit so much is to admit a good deal; it is to admit that not all epochs are equally available for the language of art, and that though we exist in our own time, it may be the part of wisdom and good taste to derive our artistic speech from another period. When Molière's hero pronounces his scorn of artificial verse and contrasts with it an old song of the people, he is rejecting a fashion that was contemporary and temporary for one that was lasting. When Homer wrote of ancient Troy, or when Æneas sang the founding of Rome, either poet was choosing the date of his story with the same taste with which he selected his theme, or selected the words of which to make his lines; he was choosing what the race after long reflection had realized was dignified, noble and true in feeling. The poet, whoever he was, that left us the *Song of Roland,* no doubt was expressing a sentiment toward France which flourished in his own day, and which may have been very foreign to the feelings of the original Roland; as in the other instances, the old story had to be changed and expurgated to make it altogether the vehicle of contemporary experience; yet he was right in taking the great figure of Roland for the outer clothing or language of his emotions, since heroic sentiments had already connected themselves with

Charlemagne's peer, as they had not yet with William of Normandy, nor with his immediate predecessors. In English history there have been efficient and picturesque rulers in plenty, yet the poets were right who have retold their national epics in the story of Arthur rather than in the biographies of Alfred or Edward I or Cromwell; for the Arthurian legend as the race has chosen to remember it is of richer fabric emotionally and of a simpler structure than any nearer and more actual history could well be. Theodore Roosevelt, for all we know, may have been a greater man than Cromwell, and time may make him seem more significant, but if the poet wishes to say things about the strenuous life, he had better say them now through the image of Cromwell, about whom our emotions are more classified; better still if he says them through the image of King Arthur, who much more than Cromwell has become a precise symbol in the imagination. Arthur was to have been the hero of Milton's epic—at least, Milton considered him for a possible hero but discarded him in favor, not of Cromwell or Hampden, but of Adam; and again the choice was wise, since Adam is still an image more universally understood than any of Milton's contemporaries, and we know what we are expected to feel when we hear his story.

To say then that in writing, even when our purpose is art and not satire, we should express ourselves in terms of the life about us, is to lay down a formula which has been contradicted in practise by the influential writers of the world. To find a language already wide-spread and therefore intelligible, the artist will always draw to some extent on the past, even though he does so unconsciously, and how far he goes back into the past will depend on what it is he wants to express. In *Henry Esmond,* Thackeray used the age of Marlborough to express a flavor of romance that could not be said in life of a later date. But when he had satire for his purpose, as in *Vanity Fair,* he chose a period comparatively modern. It is but fair to observe, however, that Thackeray follows this principle with very uncertain skill. The period he chose for his great satire was somewhat more remote than for *Pendennis* or *The Newcomes,* where his purpose was less obviously and exclusively moral; the resulting effect in each case is somewhat peculiar, since most of us, unless we count up the dates, perhaps get the impression that *Vanity Fair* was the contemporary book. In one sense it makes little difference, and we might use the illustration to indicate that it is the method of treatment, rather than the life portrayed, that will make a book seem contemporary. But we are left to wonder also whether Thackeray did not intend *Vanity Fair* to be more satirical in its effect than it actually is, and *The Newcomes* to be less so. Did the great but easy-going artist make here a careless choice of the time for his story?

Even the writers who seem now to have been most contemporary were really not so; what seems contemporary in them are eternal aspects of life, which even in their day were old. We sometimes doubt the value of those scholarly labors which search out for us the sources, so-called, of the great poets, the residuum of earlier times which they adapted to express their genius; but these labors would be justified sufficiently by the answer they give to those who think that art speaks through contemporary life. They think that we should look in our heart and write, as Sidney did, or return directly to nature, as did Wordsworth, forgetting that when Sidney looked in his heart to write, he wrote some masterly translations and paraphrases of earlier Italian or French poems, and that when Wordsworth drew on his personal experience, as in the immortal lines to the Cuckoo, he recast an earlier fine poem by Michael Bruce. The believers in the contemporary urge us to paint the record of our own times as immediately as Chaucer wove his neighbors into the tapestry of the Canterbury Tales; they do not know how many versions there were of the famous tales before Chaucer shaped them to his own purposes. Indeed, so much of the past has gone into all that we now are or say or do, that the attempt to detach ourselves from the best that has gone before is in a way a denial of contemporary character to our own times, or to any other period; for the quality of civilization in 1923 which distinguishes it

from civilization in 1823 is the gift, for
good or evil, of the hundred years in between; and to be contemporary with any
moment in history is to be aware of all the
past that still is articulate in that moment.

III

If a writer fails to use the past as the language with which to express his present, the reason may be that he does not know the past, or that he has theoretical objections to using it so, even though the great writers have followed no other method. But this reason is rarely the true one. Today as at other times any sincere writer will be interested in the great examples of his art, and will find them out, and probably the same instincts will eventually show themselves in his work as in the work of his predecessors. Undoubtedly there are poets and novelists today who through a mistaken cult of the natural are striving for a strictly contemporary utterance—rejecting, that is, all that they can recognize in our speech as having a history. If their scholarship were more complete, they would have to reject even the meagre vocabulary of word, image and legend they are now content to use. But the writer who willingly would avail himself of the full inheritance in his art finds himself limited perhaps for another reason—he finds that his readers do not know the past, that many of them cultivate an ignorance of it, and that, therefore, if he uses it to speak with, he may not be understood. It is part of the discipline which every art imposes on those who practise it, that they must speak in terms intelligible to their audience. It remains to ask, of course, who are the audience? and the writer, if he is sufficiently courageous, stubborn, or hopeful, may choose to address a more intelligent audience than he finds in his day, an audience who he thinks will at last recover the traditional tongue in which he speaks, and for whom it will be worth his while to wait. This may seem to some of us the only way out, but we know it is a precarious way. Such a brilliant belated justification came to the Greek classics at the Renaissance; it has come in music to such a giant as Bach, who was, as we say, ahead of his own day; but to expect it to come to us merely because our contemporaries do not appreciate us is entirely too obvious a self-flattery. The sane artist will rather do his best to say what he has to say in language his day understands, and he will try also to encourage his audience in the recovery of a larger language, so that he may say more to them.

This question whether the reader has sufficient command of the inherited language of literature is always an acute one for the author; the lasting successes in literature have been made at those moments when a knowledge of the past was wide-spread, and the audience were as familiar with the older literature as the writers were. Historical as Virgil seems to us in the *Æneid,* almost antiquarian, he offered to his first readers nothing they were not familiar with, and little that would not immediately kindle an emotion. In one sense then he may be said to have spoken in a contemporary language. But neither he nor his audience would have understood the doctrine that art becomes great by being contemporary, and that it becomes contemporary by discrediting the past. "To have great poets, there must be great audiences too", said Whitman, and here, as elsewhere, we are coming to realize, he got at the permanent truth of the matter. For it is a sound observation of literary historians that a country exercises its impulses toward art, in any period, as much

by what it reads of the older books as by
what it writes; the two activities must go
together if the contemporary great writer
is to get a competent hearing, and they
must be studied together if we are to estimate justly the culture of an epoch. In
what was produced, some decades of the
eighteenth century in England look to us
destitute of poetry, but in those very moments Spenser, Shakespeare and Milton
were widely loved, and enjoyed perhaps a
more humane and significant treatment
from the critics than they have often had
since. The weakness of contemporary
poetry in Addison's time, in Warton's
and Gray's, was not that they knew the
elder masters, but that their practise de-
parted so widely from them and became
so contemporary. The revival in the romantic age was brought about by rejecting the kind of art the early eighteenth
century wrote, and by building on the still

earlier art the eighteenth century had the wisdom to love.

In our day and in our land the question of the audience is peculiarly acute, and it has been rendered more so by the intentional efforts of those who believe that literature should be contemporary. Even without those efforts we, who come from many countries, with different race memories and with the legacy of different cultures, should have had difficulty enough to achieve a common language adequately rich in the best things of the past and welded into some continuity with our American future. If we write in those terms which to an Italian would be emotional, we shall hardly stir the pulses of a Scotchman or a Slav, and if we waken the race-memories of the Spanish or the French, we may leave quite cold the Dutch in Pennsylvania or the Swede in Minnesota. Our first hope, to which some of us

[164]

still desperately cling, is that we may lose
no one of these racial inheritances, but that
by a jealous conserving and study of each
of them, and by teaching them all to our
children, we may build up one of the
richest cultures that the accidents of mi-
gration have ever permitted the race to
compose. The literature of America in
a thousand years would carry in its majestic overtones the essential beauty of all
the civilizations that have made their entry
through our ports, the essential beauty too
of the wonderful Indian civilizations
which our European coming dispossessed,
and above these overtones, perhaps, the
far-off suggestions of the Greek and
Roman worlds and the immemorial East.

But this hope, whether or not it could
be realized, is so far as we can see at present a fantastic dream; our progress toward it has been slight—better, to be
frank, we have made no progress, rather

we have lost ground. There is less general culture of that sort in the United States now than there was fifty years ago. It has seemed wise to many of us, therefore, to moderate our hopes, and to aim at mastering, not all our heritages in common, but at least one tradition, and that the tradition of this country from the revolution till the present day. Such a program might be carried out in our schools—not in the colleges, since only a fraction of the country's youth gets to college, but in those early school years through which all the boys and girls may reasonably be expected to pass; and there would be nothing illogical in burdening the schools with the task, for the training of a common consciousness, cultural or otherwise, in a land of immigrants is the chief problem of elementary education. We thought, then, that we might all absorb our own past and the few decades that preceded our coming, so that hereafter the spokesmen of the nation, poets, dramatists, preachers, statesmen, might at least touch some common chords in us all by naming those who built up the opportunities we enjoy. This program is still in force in other departments of study than literature, but the teachers of literature have been largely won over to the cult of the contemporary; so far from building up in the land a great audience for the great poets to sing to, many energetic teachers of literature are persuading these children, if persuasion is necessary, to read only books of the day, about things of the day, and by inference to neglect as really negligible anything written yesterday or written about other times and other problems than ours. Our dream of a cosmopolitan culture has shrunk in practise to an educational discipline which will make us more insular and provincial than we are already, more selfish, more contemptuous of other times and of other peoples, and still further disinherited from great art.

The movement began a few years ago in a protest against the narrow choice of books permitted by the requirements for entrance to college. Some of the schools thought they could do their best work if their teachers—and their pupils—could select the books for this arduous study; there could be some wise consulting of taste, some adaptation to special temperaments. So long as the choice was still to be made from books of recognized merit, it was unreasonable to deny this request. But the trend toward the contemporary developed quickly; if we consulted the taste and the temperament of our students, the children of many racial traditions, we found that few of the older writers were easy for them to understand; the difficulty of bridging over the gap between traditions was too great for many of our teachers to solve, or perhaps they themselves were not at home in the tradition either of the books or of the students; and the most graceful form of surrender was to study only what was easy for everybody. The process was paralleled in society outside of the schoolroom, in the change in ideals and in competence which overtook professed criticism in our reviews; but the heart of the matter was and still is in the centers of education.

A teacher of English in New York City recently presented the case for contemporary literature vs. the classics, in some such argument as this: When she was in college, she said, the faculty took such an inhospitable view of the world about them that only one author, of all those they studied in literature classes, was still alive when they studied his books. She and her fellow students felt somehow cramped and cheated, not to be studying more books of which the authors were still living. In other words, whereas the critics in Mr. Shaw's play could not judge the work till they knew who wrote it, these lovers of the contemporary could not estimate a book till they knew whether the author was in or out of the graveyard. In these better days, the teacher went on to say, she and her colleagues allow for the natural desire of their students to read what is written at the moment—a life of a prominent man like Theodore Roosevelt, the work of a columnist in the daily press, the popular plays, the most talked-of novels. Such reading, she explained, gives opportunity for ethical or social or political discussion in class; she meant, it seems, that you can argue whether the Middle West was fairly portrayed, and if so, what should be done to cure it, or whether we should have gone into the war at all, or if so, what should have been done to make the lot of the private easier, and establish the officer on a less privileged plane. Out of this open discussion of spontaneous interest in current events, will come, she thought, a finer taste for the best in art.

It is obvious that the training, such as it is, which is to produce this finer taste is a training not in art at all, but in Americanization, if you choose to call it so, in sociology or in politics. These purposes are good in their place, but if they usurp the classroom where literature as an art should be taught, we need expect no aid from the schools in training us to a common culture, not at least so far as the word applies to poetry, to romance, to the drama, to the novel. We might Americanize ourselves in literature by reading our older poets—three of them, Whitman, Poe and Emerson, of influence in the whole world today; we might read our elder novelists, two of whom, Cooper and Hawthorne, at their best were among the prose-poets of the nineteenth century; or we might read Parkman, an historian not likely to be surpassed for the beauty of his spirit, for the solidity of his method, and for the romantic charm of his subject, by any who will hereafter write about this land. We might read Lincoln, about whom we talk so much, and we might profitably read Jefferson and Hamilton. We might even discover the charm of the colonial records, north and south, and the heroic poetry of our frontier, as it pushed through wilderness and across plain and canyon, to face at last the Orient again and our inscrutable future. This kind of Americanization would produce class discussion of some dignity, even though it had nothing to do immediately with the art of literature, for it would give us, not

[172]

only a sense of our common destiny, but
an escape from our own circumstances
into other days and other minds, and it
would cultivate the sympathy and the
imagination once thought to be the fruit of
literary study. But to discuss always and
exclusively only what is under our own
noses, to study a life of Mr. Roosevelt not
because it is a great biography but because
it is about Mr. Roosevelt, and to study
novels not because they are good novels,
but because they are about us, is to find
ourselves in the end just where we were
in the beginning, with our prejudices more
firmly rooted and our skin a bit thicker
to any joy or sorrow in the world not
our own. As for the ability to understand
great writing when it comes to us, we
have learned only this, that since Mr.
Roosevelt lived nearer our day than Dr.
Johnson, the biography of him is a better
biography and a more interesting one than

THE LITERARY DISCIPLINE

Boswell could write, and we need not read Boswell; and since Main Street is nearer to us than Salem, Mr. Lewis is a greater novelist than Hawthorne, and we need not read Hawthorne. Enough to know that the whole contains the part.

IV

Well, then, says the teacher of current
literature, there never can be any great
books, for you approve of nothing contemporary, and every book, unfortunately,
has to be written in its own time. Yes,
in a sense, anything you write, on however remote a subject, will be of your time
and will represent it; Walter Pater was
expressing one phase of Victorian England when he wrote *Marius the Epicurean.*
But the artist hopes to appeal to more
than the present generation; even the most
contemporary of our contemporaries, who
read no books of which the authors are not
living, cherish some ambition to have their
own works read after they themselves are
gone. And since the fame of a book de-

pends on its ability to meet the interest of
readers over a long period of time, the life
of our works will depend on two things—
on our gift for selecting the matter which
is permanently interesting to men, and
on the willingness or unwillingness of any
generation to be interested in the same
things as its predecessors. If readers are
now brought up to neglect as a matter of
course any works of literature that once
were loved, there will be no fame for any
one hereafter, and no masters of the art,
but only in each publishing season a nine
days' wonder. But if human nature still
asserts its primal interests, in spite of mistaken teaching, and continues to like in
the long run the same things that have
been loved in the past, then the writer will
finally be reckoned great who answers, not
the mood of his hour, but the spirit of those
constant demands. He will get his in-
spiration from life as he knows it; he will

express it in an eternal form, as we say
—at least in a form so durable that instead
of our understanding his work through
the incident that inspired it, we shall know
of the incident through the work. Molière
has so immortalized one moment of his
times in his *Précieuses Ridicules;* without
the play, would we know much of the temporary affectation? And to be quite
frank, has not something died in the play,
along with what was contemporary in it,
so that we enjoy it now with an historical
effort not needed to be at home, let us say,
with Falstaff? Tennyson really immortalized the Charge of the Light Brigade,
for the incident on so many grounds has
since proved regrettable that we should
be glad to forget it, but for the poem, and
we begin to be sorry that the poem is
anchored to so much that was transitory.
Our own civil war poet, Henry Howard
Brownell, true genius if we ever had one,

wrote his verses on the very scene, after the fights he had passed through as Farragut's secretary on the flagship, and the virulence of contemporary passion is in his work forever, an embarrassing alloy. But of the danger of being contemporary, Dante is the great illustration. It is not hard to see what an impact his great poem must have made on his first hearers, it was so immediate in its reference to persons, places, incidents, crimes and disasters which Florence, Rome and Italy well knew; but what an effort it is now to recover all those allusions to the times, indeed how impossible! We wrestle with them, if at all, because the greatness of the poem bears up their leaden weight; and the poem is great for what is least contemporary in it, for the vision which Dante drew from his masters, and which he handed on to the future in images of the past.

THE CULT OF THE CONTEMPORARY

The impulse to be contemporary is in our time, and perhaps always was, an impulse to tell the news. This impulse is felt perhaps in all the arts, but most in books and in the theatre, less in music, still less in painting, and least in architecture and sculpture. From these last we can learn, if we need a reminder, what are the conditions of enduring art, and what, in contrast to popularity, is fame. Sculpture and architecture, from the substantial nature of their medium, must submit to be looked at more than once, to be lived with, finally to be judged by the good opinions of many men over a long period of time; and a good opinion of such work, so lived with, will depend less on the first impression than on habitual contact. For such work popularity is difficult, if not impossible. A book about the war may be a popular book; the Farragut statue in Madison Square is not a popular statue.

What statue is popular? It can have only
the better kind of success, if any; like the
Farragut, it can be famous, loved and
returned to over an indefinite length of
time. For we can read a book once and
throw it aside, or hear music or see a play
but once, and then criticize it; it lies entirely in our choice whether we shall read
or hear twice. How different our criticism would be if it were based on at least
half a dozen readings and hearings! But
the bronze and the building are not easily
removed or ignored, and even the painting
has a good chance of being looked at more
than once. It is not surprising then that
the sculptor, like the architect or the
painter, attends to the conditions on which
fame is secured, since popularity is denied
him, and makes his appeal to revised judgments and to second thoughts.

It would be a misfortune to seem to say
that the author who misses popularity is

necessarily an artist, or that even temporary success is not to be admired. But
in American letters we are beginning to
wonder why our great successes are so
transitory; why a writer who sells more
copies of his first book than did Thackeray
or Dickens, does not continue like them
to reach a large public with succeeding
books; and why he does not, like them,
continue to be read after he has ceased to
write. The explanation suggested is that
most American writers, not only today but
throughout the last twenty-five years,
have written as journalists—have put out
their material not as life but as news about
life, and the critics have discussed it as
news, and the readers have come to look
for the news in it, and for nothing else.
Some novelists still writing began their
work with successful stories of local color,
which we read in order to learn about
Louisiana or Pennsylvania or the Middle

West, and having got the information we were looking for, we went elsewhere to look into other novelties. It goes without saying that in this process we readers have done injustice to many a work of art; *Old Creole Days* and *Main Traveled Roads* have something for the permanent reader, as well as for the news-seeker, and *Trilby* —to speak of an English book—is still a magnificent romance of friendship and chivalry, though it expired of its own success as a bulletin from the Latin Quarter and a document in hypnotism.

At least, says again the lover of current things, you must write in the language of the hour. Some beauty is lost when the poet does not speak in his native tongue, or when we cannot read him in it. Well, some languages are better than others; Greek was a better language, more precise, more varied, more forceful and more colorful, than English or any of the modern tongues. But all language changes, as the works of art in language do not; in literature we have this haunting paradox, that through a temporary medium we can build something imperishable. Much as we may dislike literature in translation, it is perhaps salutary to remember that literary masterpieces must survive in translation or not at all. In what language were the parables spoken? If Homer were not Homer still in English or French or German, how much of Homer would the world know? Some bouquet of his own time is gone, but perhaps we should not have liked it if it had remained. At least we have kept what we liked; we have kept what suited our spiritual needs, we have loved Andromache and Hector, and wondered in the old way why such fine men as Achilles and Agamemnon should quarrel, and have decided, as all our fathers have done, that for so beautiful a woman as Helen to waste her time on so mean a fellow as Paris, there must have been queer influences at work. To live in art in this timeless way, is to satisfy what is eternal in ourselves; it is to leave behind us the limitations of our hour, our place, and our language. And unless art is wide enough for us to live in it so, we shall trifle with it only for an hour, and without regret let it go the way of other contemporary things.

THE CHARACTERS
PROPER TO LITERATURE

V

THE CHARACTERS PROPER TO LITERATURE

I

OUR impulse might be to say that any character at all is proper to literature, or to any phase of literature, for we have long ago discarded that convention of ancient story which introduced the hero and heroine always as nobly born, or if at first they were not gentlefolk, yet in the last chapter they were shown to be prince and princess in disguise. Our leading characters now may have whatever origin God wills; the author does not interfere. No longer do we reserve the peasant, the poor or the ignorant for the foot of our

list of *dramatis personœ,* nor do we smug-
gle them into the scene at resting moments, for comic relief. Since human nature is the subject of art, and since the
Almighty (we quote Lincoln for this)
showed us where to put the emphasis in
human nature, by creating common folk
in the vast majority, we have even followed the example with an excess of enthusiasm, until the elect are pretty well
put down from their former seat in literature, and in their stead are the socially
humble and the mentally weak. For a
hundred years or more we have been pressing this charitable revolution. Wordsworth, though not the first to try it, first
won a considerable hearing in English
poetry for the beggar, the pedlar, the af-
flicted, the half-witted—a hearing for
them, that is, as central figures in the
poems where they occur; and shortly
afterwards the novelists, on the irresistible

tide of humanitarianism, invited not only our attention but our admiration for persons who hitherto had seemed obscure and unfortunate. Dickens perhaps went too far, we now feel; he demonstrated the weakness of the gentry, and sent them to the background of the story, where we are willing enough they should remain, but he also tried to endow the lower classes with so much delicacy, tact, and spirit that his leading persons seem to be gentry still, masquerading in a temporary eclipse of fortune, like the lost prince and princess of the fairy tale. But he taught us how to carry on his unfinished revolution; since he stripped sentimentality, all that sort of nonsense, from the gentry, we have known at last how to strip it from the bourgeois. Some of our novelists riddle the polite world for us, others tell us the unflinching truth about our middle classes. We have no heroes; any character can get into our

[189]

literature, if we may use him as a target rather than worship him as a god.

It is too late to return, even if we desired to do so, to the sentimental misreading of social conditions against which our modern realism, however grim, tries honestly to protest, and there is a form of discourse in which human frailties can properly be discussed; social science or the science of ethics would neither of them deserve the name of science if we excluded from their consideration any aspect of human character or conduct—just as medicine would fail in its office if we forbade it to study any part or function of the body. But it is not too late to ask ourselves the difference between science and art; between a story which represents our physical actions with that conscience in detail which would aid a medical diagnosis, and a story through which Helen's body walks, a joy forever; between a rec-

ord of our neighbors just as they are, or
a bit meaner, and a picture of men and
women as we would gladly be. Anything
printed may be called literature, even last
year's time-tables, but if we preserve in
the word an emphasis upon art rather than
upon information, we may ask after all
whether certain characters, or certain attitudes toward character, are not essential
to art; or, putting it another way, we
may ask whether the type of character we
portray will not determine the kind of art
we produce, with or without our will, and
whether the kind of character we portray
will not finally classify our writing for
us as art or as social document.

To have our novel appraised as a social
document may seem to us a compliment,
and we may be glad to escape the equivo-
cal verdict that our picture of life is art.
The terms are unimportant and our prejudices in words may be respected. But the

fact remains that some books we are to read many times, and permanently, whereas others are for a season only, and may be read but once; and books which must serve us in ways so different would seem to need certain special privileges of method and material—they may even be permitted certain varieties of emphasis not usually found in life. The temporary writing helps us on our way, and we ought to have one honorable name for it all— newspapers, telephone directory, time-tables, all our telegrams and most of our letters. We stop over them only for a moment, in order to go about our business more conveniently. But the other kind of books will detain us forever, or will try to—and this kind of literature is art; we return thither for no information and for no immediate aid in our daily affairs, but rather to taste again an experience we enjoyed before, to meet old friends, to breathe an atmosphere which we crave, and which is hard to find elsewhere.

If this distinction needs often to be made between the literature which is information and the literature which is art, it is because both kinds of book use the same medium, and speech is the commonest of mediums. Painting or music escape such a confusion, but writing is a slippery craft, now running to a bare record or to good advice, now drifting into a music of words, articulating a beauty that seems ageless and impersonal, and sometimes doing a bit of all these things at once. In daily conversation, when we talk of anything in human interest, we use the same words as literature is made of; what more natural than to conclude that literature therefore may deal with any subject we talk of? We resent the suggestion that art should be narrower than life itself. Yet if we admit any difference at all be-

THE LITERARY DISCIPLINE

tween art and life, between literature and
our average conversations, between books
which give information and books which
give delight, and if art is the record of
that aspect of life we delight in not for
the moment but permanently, then art
is indeed narrower than life itself; outside of it will remain the trivial things,
however likable, of our daily round,
which we forget gladly, so many other
pleasant and trivial things supplant
them; and outside of it also will remain
very important issues which we hope and
resolve shall be temporary—the grave
wrongs and errors which call not for
eternal contemplation but for reform.
Face to face with such problems, we often
feel that art is inadequate. What can
poetry do for the sick or the dying? What
solace is there in music or sculpture for
the wretchedly poor? The answer to such
questions is not in art but in conduct;

death calls for fortitude, sickness must be cured, poverty must be relieved; and if books deal with such subjects, it is not for a literary end, but to aid us in practical remedies. Indeed, to have a literary ambition as we contemplate another's misery, would seem possible only for a fiend; it is in the merit of Mrs. Stowe's story of Uncle Tom that the book seems a protest from the soul rather than a work of art. If there are sins and misfortunes, it may be necessary to spread the news, as though the house were on fire, but if we really care for our house we shall not linger to enjoy the cadence of the thrilling call. On the other hand, if we are to lose ourselves in a book or a play, if we are to live in it repeatedly, ourselves the hero, in love with the heroine, and hating the villain, then the book or play must give us an experience in some sense better than the life ordinarily available to us; who would waste a moment on Cleopatra in a book, if he knew where to find her in the world? Or perhaps in life she was less charming than Plutarch said she was, or than Shakespeare showed her to be; perhaps we could not be drawn irresistibly to her until the poet made her better than she was—made her, that is, a character proper for the literature which is to be enjoyed as art.

II

The effect of the excellence or the inferiority of the character on the book was long ago observed by Aristotle, when he said that tragedy and the epic—that is, all serious literature—will aim at representing men as better than in actual life, and that comedy and satire will represent them as worse. In this second kind of writing, he added, satire came first, and it was Homer who laid down the principles of comedy, by dramatizing the ludicrous instead of composing personal satire. This famous observation of the ancient critic has been too often read as doctrine, as though Aristotle were telling us what should take place in literature, whereas he is recording what actually does

take place. If you wish to write a story or
a play in which the reader can lose himself
with delight, you must portray character
better than the reader, character which
in some degree satisfies and strengthens
his aspirations. If you wish the reader
to laugh at the world, or to scorn it, or
to feel the need of improving it, you portray for him character in a condition inferior to his estimate of himself; if you
wish him to profit by that wholesome self-
observation which we call the comic-spirit,
you mingle satire with tragedy—you show
him character which satisfies his aspirations, so that he will identify himself with
it, and which at the same time is inferior
in some respects to what he would prefer
to be, so that he must laugh at himself.
He will have a tendency to save the day for
self-respect by laughing, not at himself,
but at human nature, and the universal
comic spirit will then have come to birth,

akin to both satire and tragedy, but more nearly a dramatizing of the ludicrous, as Aristotle said, than a scoring of personal faults.

These principles, it goes without saying, are not accepted by writers today; the average author is not aware of them, or if he is, he takes refuge in another remark of Aristotle's, that perhaps tragedy was destined to develop into something different from the type of poetry produced by Aeschylus, Sophocles and Euripides; perhaps new principles, we say, in the too familiar formula, are needed for new material. So think many of our poets and novelists who give us sordid and wretched characters to contemplate, yet invite us to feel toward them not the satiric regret, but the old pity and terror of noble tragedy. That the principles do persist, however, very much as Aristotle described them, is evidenced by the difficulty the readers still have with such books; the authors argue their case, or critics argue it for them, but common humanity remains unconvinced that misery is a proper subject for permanent contemplation. In our age especially, when the impulse to social good works is highly developed, it is a curious paradox that writers should expect us to associate in art, as habitual companions, with types of character which in real life we should hasten to rescue and to change. It is generous of the writers to suppose that in a humane age the reader will be ready to discern the heroic even beneath handicaps and afflictions, and probably the reader is thus ready, but the writers forget that in any age, particularly in a humane one, we do not like to contemplate, in the permanence of art, heroic character smothered beneath handicaps and afflictions. And in justice to the embarrassed reader it should be added that often the character is not heroic at all, and the only claim put forth for it is that it might have been attractive if it had not been smothered.

Perhaps it is the influence of Wordsworth that still spreads this confusion in our writing. The effect of many of his best known poems has never been wholly satisfactory, not even to his admirers; he drew moral lessons from objects humble or mean, and since his own interest was in the moral lesson, he sometimes was careless of the emotional appeal which the object, left standing as it were in the poem, might make on the reader. In one sense he was not a nature-lover, though he had recourse to nature for ethical wisdom; it was only the wisdom he cared about, and we have an unpleasant impression, which perhaps does him injustice, that when he had got a moral idea out

[201]

of the primrose by the river's brim, he was through with the primrose for the day. The same impression, unfortunately, is made by his portrayal of humble or mean characters. He obviously does not identify his better fortunes with their misery, nor does he enter dramatically or imaginatively into their lives; he is content to draw a moral from them, and the reader, in his day and still in ours, is surprised that misery in the picture, having produced a moral, is promptly dropped as though of no further concern. The old leech-gatherer serves a purpose when his courage against frightful odds cheers up a moodish poet; the old beggar at the door moves us to gratitude that another man's poverty keeps fresh in us our springs of charity. Much good this does the leech-gatherer or the beggar! And if there is to be no help for them, their presence is a bit disturbing in the background

of so much complacence. We wish there
were more tenderness in these poems that
talk so much of feeling. And when
Wordsworth deliberately sets out to enlist
our admiration for the heroic, we may find
ourselves facing such dumb human misery
as we have in *Michael,* the heroism of a
wrecked family and an abandoned farm.
With relief we turn to the passages in
the *Prelude* where the poet no longer
looks down benignly on the wretched, but
gives expression to the ideal life which he
himself desires to attain; there, where he
shows life better than it is, we can go with
him and lose ourselves in the vision.

It is our poets who chiefly defy Aristotle's wise warning, and try with Wordsworth to convert into a theme for medi-
tation what is really a subject for philan-
thropy. Our novelists tend more and
more to give us an inferior world, but not
for our admiration; we may smile at it,

or despise it, or try to cure it. This is satire, an achievement in morals rather than in art, and from the advertisements on the book covers it is clear that the publisher at least knows that the author is revealing something medicinal, something unpleasant but good for us. If we prefer to write satires, we are at least achieving our ambition. But the reader of the American novel today, whether he reads Mrs. Wharton, or Sinclair Lewis, or whether he goes back to an earlier period and reads W. D. Howells, is usually reading about other people, rarely about himself; he has noticed those faults in his neighbors before. We have to go far back in our literature to find a novel in which the American future is implicit, a story into which we can enter as into a world we are glad is ours. Perhaps we must go back as far as the *Scarlet Letter,* in which a modern audacity of thought seems breaking through an antique repression, and we can identify profound speculations of our own with the wisdom in Hester's heart or Arthur Dimmesdale's. It has been pointed out before how much Hawthorne gained by making his chief characters noble in the Greek way, tragic characters better than in actual life; for the sin of the woman and the minister was common enough in the world among weak or vulgar characters, and the impulse even in Hawthorne's time might well have been to keep the story, for purposes of edification or realism, in the low tone in which it first occurred. But we cannot easily take to heart the sins of people who are obviously our inferiors; only the sins of good people rouse in us tragic pity or terror, for that is the kind of sin, if any, we should commit. Hawthorne therefore makes the minister a saint, and if Hester is not a saint at the beginning, she is so at the end of her ordeal, and in the sufferings of both our own heart has been wrung. In the *House of the Seven Gables,* however, the reader is a looker-on rather than an actor, for the characters are not better than life, their experience is therefore not ours, and since we cannot cure their unhappiness, we are sorry to watch it. In that story our greatest romancer was on the road toward the modern habit of satire, a road which he had marked out for us clearly enough in some of his early sketches and tales.

The trend away from the literature of art to the literature of satire is all the more remarkable in our day because the exigencies of satire compel the American to deny wholesale his better self. There might be some apparent reason for not writing in the epic or the tragic tone if in order to do so we had to assume virtues we all knew we lacked; but why make a religion of writing satire, when to do so we must conceal the few virtues we are sure we have? Mr. Howells took it to be his duty to tell the unvarnished truth about human society as he knew it, but you would not guess from his novels that America ever produced so charming a man as Mr. Howells and those literary friends of his of whom, outside his novels, he wrote lovingly. So Mr. Lewis pictures America today—leaving out of the picture the satirical criticism of America in which he leads, and so Mrs. Wharton shows us the narrower world of fashion, with no one in it so gifted, so admirably trained, as Mrs. Wharton. The best of us is hard enough to express, as Rabbi Ben Ezra knew, but how odd that we prefer not to express it, whether difficult or easy—that we deliberately conceal what we have set our hearts on. We name half a dozen characters from his plays in whom Shakespeare seems to be portraying himself, and without too subtle a discrimination we recognize ideals of our own in all of them. Pendennis seems to be Thackeray himself, and so seems Henry Esmond and Clive Newcome, and we flatter ourselves that the great novelist incorporated in those portraits some of our own best features. We—and Cervantes—are incarnated in Don Quixote.

The contrast between information and art in our books, and the tendency to stress information with a moral bent, are both thrown into sharper relief by the success of American architecture in expressing more and more a significant and lasting beauty. Nothing might seem at first more utilitarian than a building, and few things in our country seem less permanent, we have such a passion for altering. Yet art has made its greatest progress with us in architecture, and the stages of the progress have been accompanied by just such a selection and choice of subject as Aristotle's remarks about character would imply. In our cities a genuine impulse toward beauty began to show itself two decades ago in shop-windows. Where else should beauty appear but in the enterprises we care most about? Since we were lovers of business, we began to indicate the beauty that business has in our eyes. The shop-window ceased to be, what in country hardware stores it still often is, a place where samples of all the merchandise were displayed, an order card from which you could plan your purchases; it became rather a scene of loveliness to contemplate for its own sake, an attraction to hold you rooted to the spot rather than a stimulus to hurry you inside to buy. Probably the shop-windows in our great streets could not be justified now on a purely economic basis; they have been

[209]

lifted into the realm of beauty and are things to remember. But for this kind of shop-window not every article the store sells is "proper", in the Aristotelian sense; nothing ridiculous is shown, though ridiculous things are bought and sold, nothing trivial is shown, and nothing that discloses too publicly the animal conditions in which we lead our spiritual life. With a different selection of articles which the store for our convenience must sell, we might have a comic window, the sight of which would cause us to smile at ourselves, or a satiric one, which would teach us to laugh at our fellowman.

The buildings themselves, moreover, have become beautiful by expressing what we genuinely love to contemplate, and not all kinds of buildings were proper to that happy end. For mere sale and barter, any shed in the market-place might serve, but if we think of traffic in the large way

that Ruskin suggested, as something po-
tentially heroic and noble, as a feeding of
the hungry and a clothing of the naked,
as a soldierly occupying of outposts
against poverty and wretchedness, as a
campaign of conquest against nature, and
as an exchange at last of spiritual hungers
and satisfactions among men, then our
houses of business should look like temples.
So they begin to look, and only a very
blind critic here and there still fails to see
that so they should look. With our love of
traffic goes our love of travel. In this
country travel is necessary, but it is also
an ideal. Any sort of railway station will
serve as a place to buy a ticket or board
a train, and until recently almost any kind
of barracks did serve for those purposes.
But the haphazard building could not express our delight in travel, our enjoyment
of distance and speed and punctilious
arrivings and departings. The pleasant

casualness of the stage-coach and the road-side inn does not really appeal to us, except in exotic moments; our religion of travel is uttered in the Pennsylvania Station in New York, and in other such structures fast rising throughout the country, where the ritualistic atmosphere, produced by carefully selected elements from the buildings of antiquity, have little to do with buying your ticket and a great deal to do with the American spirit. We breathe more freely as we enter them, and enjoy the space and the height; our instinctive comment is, "This is something like!" as though some part of us had found expression at last. And if this success in architecture is as yet in the field of business and travel, among public buildings, the reason probably is that in those fields we know what our aspirations are. In ecclesiastical architecture, by way of contrast, we are less clear. We feel that if the Woolworth building is so lovely, it is but respectable to improve the appearance of our churches, so we put up very wonderful Gothic chapels and cathedrals— only to find, perhaps, that they are a sort of weight on our conscience rather than an expression of our desires; we sometimes try to cultivate the religion that produced them, in order that so eloquent a language may have more content in its words.

When we turn back from our architecture to our books, we have the right to ask why poetry and the novel address themselves exclusively to what is in essence satire, to the portrayal of us as worse than we are, or with our aspirations left out; why we as readers must be invited to absorb mere information about ourselves and our country; why we so seldom meet in the pages offered to us the kind of men and women we admire or ought to admire. The arts all express the same thing, at any given moment, and if we are equally proficient in them, they ought to achieve the same grandeur and the same beauty. Against the trivial and drab contents of much of our poetry and the condescending realism of much of our prose American architecture now stands, a reproach and an indictment; for the imaginative power and sweep of our buildings is hardly discernible in our books. The architects have followed old wisdom, by making their work ideal, better than life. The writers, in a stubborn wrong-headedness, in defiance of the readers' psychology, portray characters worse than in actual life, and sometimes ask us to admire them.

III

To ask what characters are proper to literature as an art, and to point out that the character better than life will express our ideals, and that the character worse than life will invite our satire, is only to raise in another way the old problems of the universal as against the particular in art, of the contemporary as against the eternal. To be strictly personal is in the end to be contemporary, and to be strictly contemporary is to give, whether or not we intend it, the effect of satire. If our picture of life is to appeal to the reader, and to many readers, as their own world, not simply as their neighbors' private house into which they are prying, it must have general human truth beyond what is

strictly personal; and if it is to be read
with that sense of proprietorship by many
people over a stretch of time, it must not
limit itself to the peculiarities of any one
moment. It is true that the writer himself lives but one life and is circumscribed
by time and place; if there were no such
thing as imagination he would only record
what he is, for the enlightenment of others
who are just like him; without imagination he would not know of a better character than his, or of a worse one, and we
should be spared the discipline of satire,
but at the price of art. The problem for
the writer, as for any other artist, is to
imagine the lives of other men, and the
lives that he and other men aspire to; his
business is to select from personal adventure what is generally important, and to
see it against the background of universal
experience. Can any one imagine universal experience? Perhaps not, but the

nearer he comes to this difficult success the more readers the world over will find meaning in what he writes. To have a personal career is no ground for conceit in an artist—every one has as much; the achievement is to state our experience so that it is the experience of other people too.

If we portray characters as better than in actual life, there is no great difficulty in making them seem universal; for it is a radical gift in human conceit to fancy that anything admirable or desirable has a possible connection with ourselves. If we do not at first discover what there is in common between Romeo or Lincoln or Achilles or General Lee and ourselves, yet if we admire them we shall find the resemblance, or try to create it. This is the power of great imaginative art, that the admirable things in it generate a kind of universal emulation, and the story or statue which has been said to imitate nature succeeds at last in persuading men and women quite naturally to imitate it. The power of a great book over human conduct, even its influence at last upon what might seem instinctive conduct, is immeasurable. In the troubadour art of love before Dante's time, a true lover was taught to turn pale at sight of his lady, and at the unexpected sight of her to faint; Dante loved that literature, and he grew pale and fainted by second nature— just as women once learned to blush at certain things, and afterward learned not to blush. How many lives were affected, for good or evil, throughout Europe and America, by the alluring power of Byron's heroes and heroines? The poet, then, who represents character as better than actual life, as possessing, that is, something that we desire but have not, has already made his hero universal,

and must some day accept the responsibility of having dedicated his readers to
that general ideal. We may question
Byron on moral grounds by asserting that
his hero, after whom so many lives were
patterned, was really not deserving of any
imitation; just as an Oriental reformer
from India might tell us that the traffic
and travel of which our architecture is an
expression are both of them trivial enterprises, mere distractions from the con-
templative ends of life. But such criticism
lies outside of art. To understand the
discipline which art imposes on us it is
enough to observe the kind of character
which does make an ideal effective in literature, and the kind that precipitates us
into satire.

The real difficulty for the writer is not,
then, in generalizing the characters which
embody his ideal, and which therefore are
better than in actual life; what he will

chiefly need for his success is to have the ideals. But even with a consciousness of deep aspiration he may wish to include in the picture whole characters or parts of character which are not what they should be, and which yet are likable, even lovable; and to give this double effect of inferiority in some sense, together with charm in some sense, is, it seems, very difficult, for this is the effect of comedy, and comedy is rare in any literature, almost entirely absent from our own. If you represent a character as worse than in actual life, the condescending attitude of the reader will not automatically draw the portrait into some universal relation; the writer must add something universally admirable to the particular weakness we look down on. Beatrice and Benedick have exhausted their wit, and they are the victims of a plot to marry them off to each other; for such inferiority to their companions we cannot admire them. But Shakespeare makes them both loyal to their friends and generous in their delight in life, and Beatrice has the good sense to know innocence when she sees it; these qualities we can identify with our own virtues, and for these we admire the hero and heroine. The poet further generalizes both characters by reminding us through their meditations that to fall in love is not the work of reason, and that even the wittiest scoffers succumb; here too we gladly recognize our own experience. We can therefore smile at the foibles of the young people, partly because these foibles are incident to all human nature, and partly because, even with the foibles, we like to identify ourselves in imagination with the supplementary virtues. Socrates was trying to persuade Aristophanes and Agathon, in the gray dawn after the Symposium, that the art of comedy and the art of tragedy are the same; and so far at least he was right, in that the universal rendering which character must receive in both, gives to the comic effect some of the pity, though none of the terror, which tragedy evokes. But Socrates did not say that the art of tragedy is identical with the art of satire.

When comedy is at its best—that is, when we have made the inferior character universal by showing that its faults are natural, or by adding to it some general virtues—we may indeed go further and say that comedy produces perhaps the terror as well as the pity of tragedy, and that the two kinds of writing are, as Socrates said, but one. The tragic or epic hero, portrayed as better than in actual life, may have faults, but so far from despising him on that account, we may not even smile; we like him so much that the faults seem his misfortune. Moreover, if

[222]

we refer the weakness of the comic character to nature itself, how can we be hard on the individual? And if we add to the faults positive and lovable virtues, will not the comic character seem at last to be tragic? In English drama Falstaff is perhaps the prince of comic characters, so vitally imagined that he lives on the stage apart from any plot; he is a living person, with no virtues at all, yet infinitely likable. He can be played to make the groundlings laugh, but most of us after we have laughed taste profound tragedy in what we have laughed at. He is almost majestic in those moments of cowardice when he portrays himself exactly as he is— when he sees himself, as it were, from outside, and points to those aspects of his frailty which belong to mankind. An actor might play the scenes on the battlefield in *Henry IV* so as to inspire, not laughter at the fat knight's depravity, but a pitiful and self-accusing silence. When he finds the corpse of Sir Walter Blunt, just slain—"Soft! who are you? Sir Walter Blunt!—There's Honour for you! Here's no vanity! . . . I have led my ragamuffins where they are peppered; there's but three of my hundred and fifty left alive, and they are for the town's end, to beg during life. . . . I like not such grinning honour as Sir Walter hath. Give me life; which if I can save, so; if not, honour comes unlooked for."

In French drama Molière brought comedy to an excellence not matched, per-haps, in any other literature, and no imaginative writing is richer than his in general ideas. We laugh at the amusing situation, or delight in the frankly arti-ficial balancing of the plot, but on second thoughts we fall silent, contemplating the universal sweep of humanity, ourselves included, which he has uncovered for us.

PROPER CHARACTERS

The most obvious example for American readers is in *Tartuffe,* where the unhappy Elmire has difficulty in proving to her husband Orgon that Tartuffe, whom he greatly admires, is a treacherous friend and is actually making love to her. She finally admits Tartuffe to her room, having first hidden her husband under the table, from which he has promised to emerge if Tartuffe should go beyond the bounds of decency. Tartuffe, of course, makes love in the clearest terms to his friend's wife, but Orgon remains concealed. "Before we go any further", says Elmire, "just look down the hall to make sure my husband isn't coming." "Why worry about him?" says Tartuffe, "we can lead him around by the nose." Then Orgon comes from under the table. Where has the comedy brought us? Is it not to a contemplation of our own vanity, the source of the sense of honor in us all?

Are we laughing at Tartuffe and Orgon, or are we thinking of ourselves?

Falstaff and Tartuffe illustrate the generalizing of inferior characters by the ascribing of their faults to human nature. A good illustration of the comic character which enlists our admiration and is a genuine ideal is Huckleberry Finn. His ignorance, his poverty, and his lack of humor would seem to disqualify him for any heroic career in literature, yet he is a veritable hero, in the sense that we gladly put ourselves in his point of view and return again and again to live for an hour or so in his experience. The reason is that along with his inferior qualities he has characteristics and he has a fortune which seem better than ours; he is loyal to Tom and the negro Jim, he has a simple faith and zest in life, and he has exciting adventures and gets romance out of scenes we should otherwise find dull. He flatters

us too by admiring people and things
which from his praise we know we should
treat satirically. To know what comedy
is, as opposed to satire, we have but to
read his story again and compare it with
any current indictment of the scene in
which his adventure was laid.

IV

If the principles of tragedy, comedy
and satire are as implicit in our psychology
now as when Aristotle described them, and
if the principles of decorum, of art, and of
the timeless ánd the impersonal in art, are
as rooted in life as they are declared to be,
there might seem to be no great need to
preach them; the practice of literature
would disclose them in spite of our ignorance. Try as we might to make a lovable
hero out of an inferior character, he would
still emerge a figure in satire or, if we
generalized his faults, a figure in comedy;
in serious literature, only a character
better than in real life would give satisfaction. Though we do not doubt that the
principles of art will thus be rediscovered

pragmatically by the unescapable discipline of literature, yet it is something of
a pity to go through such lengths of experiment in order to find out what was
known before. And the great danger in
our country is that we may not push the
experiment to the tedious but profitable
end at which sound knowledge awaits us;
we may grow weary of the discipline, and
take refuge in parody or in sentimentality.
These two avenues of escape from the
problem have cursed American literature
before, and signs are not wanting that
they now are the temptations of those
who yesterday were our "new" writers and
promised brave things. Face to face with
characters worse than in actual life, we
may find our own satiric attitude monot-
onous, but to handle such material otherwise than satirically, we must master the
art of comedy, and comedy is an art too
difficult. What Bret Harte and Riley

and Eugene Field did in such circumstances was to obscure the meanness of the subject by sentimentality, instead of illuminating it by the comic spirit. Spoon River has been celebrated before, though we may not have recognized the subject with the old sentimental surface removed; much of our contemporary satire has been the kind of surgical operation necessary to separate the American reader from the sentimentality which in his heart he likes. Since it is in his heart, he may express it again quite shamelessly, this time as a protest against too much satire, and we may have another welter of old oaken buckets and old swimming holes and little boy blues—the literature that provides the satisfaction of a good cry, without the over-exertion of tragic pity or terror. Already we have again the familiar and dilettante essay, the imitation of eighteenth-century style, even in newspaper columns, the interminable parodies of Horace, which in this country have been the advance signals of the sentimental wave.

We can but hope that the signs may prove deceptive, and that literature in America will not wait much longer for the characters and subjects proper to it, and proper to the dramatic hour we live in—characters and subjects expressing that better part of us which has given our land its direction and its power, and expressing also that other world of the spirit which man builds for elbow-room to exercise his genuine ideals in, and carries it around with him, and sets it up to be a tabernacle in the wilderness of this natural world.